Praise for
Cut, Stapled, & Mended

"Roanna Rosewood's *Cut, Stapled, & Mended* is a bold statement of our birthing times. Every woman—whether you've birthed a baby naturally or not—will find elements of themselves in her story. Please listen closely, notice how this ode to a pregnant woman's human rights is a plea many women feel too silenced to speak. Thank you Roanna for offering your voice and speaking your truth."

–Karen Rachel Brody, playwright, "Birth" and founder of BOLD

"A riveting, personal story, a true 'heroine's journey' of the author's pregnancies, motherhood and the quest for a natural birth. A deeply compelling, rigorously honest, humorous, poignant, and inspiring tale. Anyone interested in the power of natural birth, anyone planning on having a baby or in supporting someone on their journey to motherhood needs to pick this book up. And once you pick it up, you won't be able to put it down until you're wiping your eyes, sharing her joy, sharing a heart filled with her triumph."

–Sheri Winston, founder amd executive director of the Center for the Intimate Arts and author of *Women's Anatomy of Arousal*

"I blamed my midwife for my failure to progress but secretly knew it was me; my lack of confidence lead to my failure to progress. Reading *Cut, Stapled and Mended* made me realize I can start building confidence in my body, mind, and self, now. It gave me the kick in the pants I needed to start getting my life in order, my heart figured out, and my mind straight. Thank you."

–Jennifer Quarne Minsch, mother

Cut, Stapled, & Mended

When One Woman
Reclaimed Her Body
and Gave Birth
on Her Own Terms
After Cesarean

ROANNA ROSEWOOD

CONFLUENCE BOOKS
ASHLAND, OREGON

Confluence Books is an imprint of White Cloud Press

Confluence Books titles may be purchased for educational, business, or sales promotional use. For information, please write:

Special Market Department
Confluence Books
PO Box 3400, Ashland, OR 97520
Website: www.whitecloudpress.com

Cover and interior design by Confluence Book Services

Printed in the United States of America

13 14 15 16 17 18   10 9 8 7 6 5 4 3 2 1

Library of Congress Cataloging-in-Publication Data

Rosewood, Roanna.
Cut, stapled, and mended : when one woman reclaimed her body and gave birth on her own terms / Roanna Rosewood.
    pages cm
 Includes bibliographical references and index.
 ISBN 978-1-935952-77-0 (pbk.)
1. Rosewood, Roanna--Health. 2. Natural childbirth. 3. Vaginal birth after cesarean. I. Title.
RG661.R668 2013
618.4'5--dc23
                                                    2013006275

In honor of the women through whom I was born:

> My mother, Ani Nyima Dolma (1944–), daughter of
> Verna Theurer (1921–), daughter of
> Arverna Grant (1892–1963), daughter of
> Annie Mariah Hunsaker (1862–1933), daughter of
> Katherine Jensen (1843–1927), daughter of
> Annie Mariah Clawsen (?–1848), daughter of
> Anne Catherine Urbanson, daughter of . . .

And those who will be birthed through me.

With special thanks to the friend and midwife who made my story possible, Laura Roe.

Note to the Reader

In telling this story, I've changed a handful of names to protect others' privacy. Everything else is exactly the way I remember it. You won't approve of all of it. I certainly don't. If I could change my past, this would be a very different story. Tread gently through these, the pages of my life. Regardless of your stance in the birth wars, we all want the same thing: healthy and happy babies and mothers.

Contents

1 She Visits

I share a bed with my husband, Ben; our children, Avram (age three and a half) and Jonah (fifteen months); and Sky Kitty. We did not plan it this way. There was a time when I was adamantly opposed to family beds. But as each newborn, so small and sweet, came into our lives, it seemed natural to welcome him into our bed. These darling babies have grown into sprawling, long-legged, kicking, leaking, not-so-sweet-smelling boys. And over time, our bodies learned to bend and flex around them in sleep, eight arms and eight legs tangled together with four paws and a tail.

This is called co-sleeping, a term that flusters most Westerners. Elsewhere in the world, co-sleeping is common. Tactfully, people ask how we manage to get any sleep, but what they really want to know is if Ben and I still have sex.

Smiling mysteriously, I like to tell skeptics, "It just takes creativity." But that's not completely true. Most often sex involves nothing more than dropping our bodies—along with our standards—off the bed and onto the floor. Our children are heavy sleepers. While the couch would be more comfortable, it would also involve planning, or at least enough energy to get up and walk into the other room.

For now, we are into the spontaneous thing. While that sounds exciting, what it really means is that we often forget to have sex until after we fall asleep. When I feel a hand or mouth at my breast—here is the impressive part—without waking up, I determine who is doing the caressing. Jonah I bring closer, tilting my body to give him easy access to nurse. Avram I face away from me while pressing him in close, using his own body to shield my "nummies" from him. My husband . . . well, the response varies. But it rarely involves going all the way into the other room.

Though the floor is now our standard routine, last night was different. A bed was involved, and we were both wide awake. Apparently being awake is conducive to great sex, because it was great sex. A place deep inside of me, a place I didn't even know existed, was called to respond. I held back as long as I could. I held back until some other-world goddess possessed my body—for surely the extraordinary woman riding cowgirl style with her face thrown back was not me. Orgasmic Amazon Queen had taken over, her hands running over my body and through my hair, her voice filling the room, leaving the person previously known as me lying there speechless.

It's not often that I find myself without words. Then again, I had never before been possessed by a goddess. Like a fish, my mouth opened and shut. When sound finally passed through it, I heard the last words I could have imagined myself saying: "I'm pregnant."

"It's a girl," Ben replied, and just like that he fell asleep.

What kind of time is this to fall asleep? Does he realize what he just said? Why would he say it unless he, too, experienced some strange thing? If he did, what was it?

As the endorphins wore off, my normal brain regained control and lectured me.

Get it together. You are not someone who gets all woo-woo goddessy or stuck in feelings. You are rational; there is no reason to think you are pregnant. Your only two conceptions were well planned. Both times, you found out the normal way, with a pregnancy test. No weird hunches or cosmic energy was involved.

I am not a New Age sort of person. In fact, I am anti–New Age, probably because my parents tried to raise me to be New Age. In their home, we slept on futons and ate seaweed, tofu, and brown rice daily. Tai Chi, moxa, yoga, meditation, yin and yang, alternative healing, and philosophical discussions were the norm. As a result, once I left home, I did my best to avoid all things New Age.

I'm not saying that numerology, crystals, palm reading, channeling, and psychics are bogus. They are simply irrelevant. I prefer coffee to mate, the internet to astrology, and deodorant to patchouli. I don't care what color my chakras are. I create my own future and have enough to do in my busy exterior life that I don't see reason to analyze the inner one.

Rationally, for I pride myself in always being rational, I conclude that the whole goddess experience was not real but the result of great-sex-meets-too-much-spicy-food. I resolve to not think about it again and, wrapping my arms around Ben's peaceful body, join him in sleep.

When morning comes, there is no time for indulgent baby girl thoughts. My boys, still in various stages of undress, have turned the couch into a fortress and are whacking each other with pillows. Sky hides from the commotion under a table, the tip of his tail twisting in disapproval.

I make breakfast, wrestle the boys into clothing, feed them oatmeal with butter and maple syrup, change their sticky, syrup-covered clothing, do dishes, fold laundry, put the couches back together, get the boys into their raincoats and rubber boots—a must in our Oregon spring—herd them out the door, and buckle them into their car seats to take them to their annual well child exams.

The kids' room at the doctor's office is decorated with animal pictures. Jonah reaches for a colorful seahorse mobile. Avram wants me to read an animal board book. Dutifully, I make animal noises: "bahhhh," "mooo," "woof woof." In between noises, I answer the doctor's routine questions.

"No, no concerns about their health. Meow. Yes, they are still nursing. Oink, oink! No, no thumb sucking. Gobble gobble. Be careful, Jonah, soft with the pretty seahorse. No, we don't really drink a lot of juice. Maybe a couple of times a week. I don't know what kind of noises sea horses make, Avram. Yes, some milk, but not much. Mostly we drink water. Here, Jonah, do you want to look at this book instead? That's right, horses say neigh. Yes, they do eat a lot of vegetables and fruit."

In the midst of these three separate conversations, my mind flashes back to the previous night. When the doctor asks, "How much sugar do the children eat?" I answer, "Can I get something to prevent conception?" Feeling my face flush, I explain, "We had a little accident last night."

This being the first time in my life I have ever uttered anything like this, I don't know what to expect. Avoiding contact with the doctor's eyes, I look back at the book and say "cock-a-doodle-doo" to Avram and "Please don't eat the sea horse" to Jonah.

Sneaking a peek at the doctor, I see that he is scribbling off a prescription. He does not look horrified, scold me for being irresponsible, or question my sex life but hands the prescription over as if it's normal. "Take this and your cycle will come as usual," he instructs.

Thanking him, I pocket it and say "roar!" to Avram.

We head next to the grocery store. Avram, pushing his own mini shopping cart, runs up and down the aisles with complete disregard for the humans and stacked displays of bottled wine in his way. Jonah, from his seat in my shopping cart, watches his big brother with envy, kicking his legs and cheering each time Avram has a near miss.

Filling the cart high with groceries, I think about how much I'm not ready to be pregnant again. Two kids are enough for now. I love my boys, but they are so much work. I have only two hands, and sometimes I need to use them both, one on each child, just to hold them back, pull them forward, or hug them close. What would I do with three kids?

A familiar "uh-oh" from the fruit area interrupts my thoughts. Avram, meaning to take just one orange, has set off an avalanche. Together we pick the oranges up. Jonah, seizing his moment of freedom, twists around to grab a box of cookies, which, with lightning speed, he opens and then begins cramming into his mouth.

Quit daydreaming of little girls. Pay attention to the children you already have.

The rest of the day passes much like every other. I feed them lunch, do dishes, and, seeing Jonah rub his eyes, read *Kiss The Cow* to him as his small body succumbs to sleep. Thinking I might use the moment to check email, I pull out the train set to entertain Avram while I pop into the home office.

When the sound of silence interrupts my work, I check on Avram. He is not where I left him in the living room, and the bathroom door is suspiciously closed. When I open it; Sky bursts out, running for his life. Avram stands in a large puddle of water, his arms and shirt covered in suds while tracks and trains float in a bubble bath. He is saved a scolding only because Jonah, choosing this moment to wake up, cries for me. I comfort Jonah and then prepare a snack of sliced apples and almond butter, to occupy their attention while I clean the bathroom. When they finish their apples, they see who can jump the farthest off the couch, each leap accompanied by an earsplitting screech. I try to distract them with an art project.

In the time it takes for a brief phone call to grab my attention, the boys unwrap each and every crayon, tearing the crayon papers into dozens of little pieces. After soaking the papers in their water cups, they scatter the pieces like confetti all over the floor. The bare naked crayons they use to color the table and walls, leaving the neat stack of white paper untouched.

While I clean up this mess, another one explodes out of Jonah's diaper. This one stinks. I change both boys' diapers while telling Avram, through clenched teeth, "Next time let's pee in the potty like a big boy!"

When the kids see Ben's car pull into the driveway, they run straight through the pile of clothes I am folding to greet him. Lifting the boys into a giant bear hug, Ben looks around at the scattered laundry, sink full of dishes, towels of drying train tracks, and smiles at me. Stooping to give me a hug, he kindly does not mention that I stink—somehow I forgot to shower—and asks me what's for dinner. I reply with a scowl, knowing full well that the bag he is holding contains wild mushroom panini and roasted garlic potato soup from our care. People say owning a restaurant is hard work, and they're right. But let me tell you, the perks are fabulous.

Ben takes over parenting duties, leaving me free to take a shower. While peeling off my jeans, a crinkly noise reminds me of the prescription in my pocket—the prescription I forgot to fill. Looking at it, I read "Plan B." It sounds so simple. I take a pill or two and my period will come as usual, assuring that, nine months from now, I will still have only two children. *I'll fill it first thing in the morning*, I think, propping the prescription up on my dresser so I won't forget it.

Tucking my sons into bed, I pat backs and sing softly: "I love you more than ever, more than time and more than love. I love you more than money and more than the stars above . . ." until their breathing deepens and Jonah's fidgeting is replaced with light snores. Downstairs in the office, a pile of paper work is waiting for me by the computer. But snuggling between the two boys is so sweet; instead I close my eyes, inviting sleep.

Except that the prescription is staring at me from across the room.

Refusing to indulge in fancies, I hold my eyelids firmly closed. But there is no hiding from my imagination; unbidden, images of a soft little girl in pink lacy clothes come to me.

Quit it! I scold myself. *If you were pregnant, which you're not, there is a fifty-fifty chance there would be no pink, lacy clothes. It could be a boy. Besides, you're not ready to be pregnant. Sometime, maybe, but not now.*

Don't misunderstand. I love my boys. It's just that the testosterone level in this house is off the charts. (Have I mentioned that our cat is also male?) Males are a fascinating species; I'm blessed to have an abundance of them in my life. But I have so many more than my share.

Scowling—is it at myself or the slip of paper?—I climb out from between the boys, walk across the room, pick up the prescription, put it into a drawer, which I close with a bit more force than necessary, and return to bed, to find that Jonah's diaper is leaking and the bedding needs to be changed.

Waking early the next morning, I ready myself for a "day off." By this I mean I'm going to work at our restaurant, Pangea, instead of filling mom duty. Dressed in my daily garb of a logo T-shirt, jeans, and restaurant clogs, with my long hair pulled back into an easy-to-manage ponytail, I kiss the boys good-bye. As I prepare to step out the door, a question from Avram stops me in my tracks, "Mom, why do you want three kids?"

Startled, and wondering what he knows that I don't, I cautiously reply, "I don't know if I do want three kids, Avram."

"Yeah huh, me and Jonah and Papa," he says.

Grinning at Ben, I tell Avram, "Because I have three such great kids and I love them so much. That's why I want three kids!"

Avram smiles proudly. Ben play-glares. I run to my dresser, grab the previously forgotten prescription, and dart out the door. Rushing to get to the restaurant in time to let the staff in, I tell myself I will fill it after my shift.

Food has always been a big part of my life. My childhood home doubled as a residential macrobiotic education center. My parents treated people—most of whom had been told by doctors that they were going to die—through dietary changes. They cured many. I was taught that food was the reason people were dying and also the means to heal them. Because my parents held little regard for doctors and hospitals, I received neither immunizations nor check-ups but grew up swaddled securely in the belief that diet, acupuncture, and Eastern medicines held the answers to all ailments.

The base of our diet was whole grains, seasonal and regional vegetables, beans, and sea vegetables. I was allowed only minimal and regionally grown fruit. We did not keep dairy, poultry, red meat, or sugar in our home. My mother made my birthday cake by cooking couscous with apple juice for sweetener and then pressing it into a pan, where it took the shape of a cake as it cooled. She frosted it with chestnut paste sweetened with a little maple syrup. I was the only kid in school who brought sushi for lunch. Mom made it with whole grain brown rice (leaving out the traditional sugar and rice vinegar) with an umeboshi (pickled unripe plum) in the middle, forming it lovingly into a heart shape for me.

Choosing what to cook was never a simple matter of deciding what one was in the mood to eat. Everything from one's emotional and physical health to the season, the weather, and the plans for the day was considered because each food has its own medicinal properties.

Take rice, for example. It generates energy, enhances digestion, relieves mental depression, quenches thirst, alleviates diarrhea, and soothes irritations from summer heat.[1] But that's not all. Rice comes in more than forty thousand known varieties—a multitude of colors, shapes, and sizes, each with its own unique gifts. Short-grain brown rice has more minerals than the long-grain variety and is preferred in cooler seasons. Basmati rice is good for overweight people. Sweet rice is warming and more easily digested than regular rice.[2] And wild rice is not usually wild at all, but quite tame, having been treated with regular doses of petrochemical fertilizers, herbicides, insecticides, and fungicides.

The preparation of rice was equally important. During cold winters, Mom would pressure-cook rice to make it more dense, digestible, and energizing. In summer, she simmered it, resulting in a fluffy, light, summery meal. Sometimes she would sprout it first; other times she would roast it.

For a special treat, we pounded sweet rice to make mochi, small balls of stretchy rice said to be excellent for pregnant and nursing women. Mochi stretches and contracts, just like a woman's body does during labor.

"When you have a baby in your belly, I will make mochi for you," my mom promised.

It's not just rice that has a story. Every grain, vegetable, fruit, bean, oil, salt, spice, and herb has its own meaning and its own method of preparation, each one as important as rice's. In this spirit, in my parents' home three meals a day were planned, made from scratch, and honored as the foundation of our bodies, not just an experience for the taste buds.

My parents were considered gurus by their community but, as a child, I was more interested in flavor than health or the greater meanings of food. I seized every opportunity to eat sugar and dairy. Other teens rebelled by drinking alcohol. I drank soda. Okay, I drank some alcohol also. But soda was serious rebellion in my family.

The only limitation on my diet was one that I had imposed on myself as a tween. On a family fishing trip, I had watched how hard the fish fought to resist the pull of the line, how it squirmed for freedom in my father's hand, and how the sharp tip of the hook pushed its way through its mouth and skull. I felt so badly for this fish that I spent the rest of the trip in tears, and I vowed to never eat an animal again. This was not particularly difficult; since fish and meat were only rarely offered in our macrobiotic home, I never missed it.

Being vegetarian became a large part of my identity. I believed that it was the morally correct thing to do and that nobody had the right to cause death in order to eat. The sight, and smell, of others eating meat repulsed me. Righteously I would explain that eating meat was unethical and bad for the world.

When I moved out on my own, I filled my kitchen with the same healthy ingredients that I had grown up with. Though I wasn't particularly interested in or skilled at cooking, every day I made at least one meal of a whole grain, bean or tofu dish, plus vegetables. Aside from that obligatory nod to my health and upbringing, I relished the freedom to eat whatever I wanted, exploring the boundaries of my taste buds the way one explores a new and highly desirable lover. I reveled in chocolate and coffee and donuts and cheese and pasta and chocolate and ice cream and macaroni with cheese and lasagna and chocolate and cheese puffs and hot cocoa and whipped cream and French fries and chocolate.

When I met Ben, a tall, handsome chef with dark hair and blue eyes, it was food at first sight. Though he was professionally trained,

Ben wasn't familiar with many of the foods in my kitchen—sea vegetables, teff, lotus root, quinoa, nattō. He didn't know that food has medicinal qualities, or that it could be valued for anything but flavor or calories. In turn, though my exotic ingredients turned him on, he was surprised that I didn't know the "right" way to hold a chef's knife or even the simplest culinary school techniques to best bring out flavors. Ben took my ingredients and cooked them in a way they had never been cooked before. Just like that, I fell in love. The more we cooked together, my ingredients and philosophy simmering in Ben's training and skill, the more obvious it became that we were meant to be together, both in and out of the kitchen.

Given our combined backgrounds in food, perhaps it's no surprise that Ben and I now own an eclectic and healthy café—to which, on this drizzly April morning, I am headed to work. Glancing at the drugstore across the street, I make a mental note to fill the prescription on my way home. Settling into my routine, I count the cash in the drawer, make coffee, and check in with the employees. Because of the rain, I put on extra soup. Today's selection: portobello bleu cheese, coconut curried yam, buffalo chili with chipotle sour cream, and wild salmon chowder.

Soon we are bustling with customers, making it easy to avoid the carefully folded slip of paper in my pocket. I make espresso drinks, pour rose lemonade, and visit with regulars. Six hours later, at the end of my shift, I square my shoulders, take a big breath, and ready myself to cross the street to the drugstore. But as I open the door to leave, a mama with a new baby snuggled close to her in a front sling enters. Holding the door for her, I sneak a peek into her sling, catching a glimpse of a little fist curled next to a soft cheek. Blinded by the sight of this sweet baby, I walk past the drug store, purposefully not glancing in its direction.

As I drive, I think of the smell of a new baby and the softness of its skin. I do not think about the prescription. At home, besieged by boys, ignoring the prescription is even easier. Avram runs around the house. Jonah, his lighter footsteps doing double time, follows his big brother everywhere. A steady stream of yelling and crashing accompanies them. The ruckus is good—anything to stop me from thinking about prescriptions and babies.

This tactic works until I find myself in bed that night trying to sleep. The voice in my head, annoyed at having been ignored all day, nags.

"You don't want to be pregnant. Fill the prescription."

Feigning deafness, I ignore the voice. This doesn't work.

"I'm just going to keep on until you answer."

"I'm not pregnant. It's not rational to think I could be," I argue back.

"Better to be safe."

"Yes, but I don't want to take drugs."

"You believe in a woman's right to choose," the voice scolds.

"But I've never chosen this before."

"Just fill the prescription . . . fill the prescription . . . fill the prescription," the voice in my head continues.

This conversation is bizarre, not because I'm arguing with myself. That's normal. What I don't understand is why I don't want to be pregnant. I would like to have another baby. What am I resisting?

2 Baby Dreams

I've wanted babies for as long as I can remember. I used to sit next to my mother as she nursed my baby brother and "nurse" my doll, dreaming of the day that the baby I held in my arms would pulse sweet milk dreams and curl her toes around the touch of my fingertips.

Even the class assignment in junior high designed to discourage early pregnancy did not dissuade me. Our homework was to carry an egg around for a week to teach us how difficult caring for a baby can be. Now that I have had two—babies, not eggs—let me say that this egg thing is a horrible idea. Caring for a baby is absolutely nothing like caring for an egg. I've spent a number of sleepless nights holding a screaming baby while cheerfully imagining myself lobbing eggs (but not babies) at the teacher who thought to correlate the two.

As a rebellious teen who didn't feel accepted or loved, I wanted a baby the way one covets a puppy from the store window. But there is no quicker way to make a young man decide he isn't ready for sex than to talk babies. How do I know? My best friend, Stella Lynn, and I went so far as to poke holes in condoms to try to get pregnant from our unsuspecting boyfriends. Relatively quickly, one of them heard us giggling about it and warned the other. They began providing their own condoms. Stella was eventually successful in her quest, giving birth to her first child at nineteen.

My only requirement in this delusional goal of getting pregnant and raising a child myself was that the donor's genetic makeup be worthy. This is probably what saved me, because I didn't have any such romantic relationship between my hole-poking days and when I met

Ben. When my period failed to come as expected six months after Ben and I began dating, I ran out to buy a test, excitedly anticipating pregnancy.

It was on the toilet, pee-covered stick in hand, that common sense hit me like a wasp on meat. Just like that, I realized that I wanted marriage first.

Luckily for us, the test came up negative.

One and a half years later, Ben and I decided to get our lives together. I was teaching horseback riding, a fairytale job that didn't exactly cover the bills. Ben, who worked sixty-hour weeks catering, made more money but had little time. I didn't want to raise children in overpopulated and crime-ridden South Florida, where we were living. So we cooked up a plan to open our own restaurant. Much to the chagrin of Ben's parents, we then quit our jobs, bought a van, and set out to find the perfect place to start a new life.

Jamming ingredients into every cranny of our van, we tested recipes on a small cook stove along the way, refining our restaurant concept to a gourmet soup, sandwich, wrap, and panini shop. We would favor seasonally organic produce while utilizing super-foods and exotic ingredients from around the world. I wanted it to be vegetarian, but Ben absolutely refused. We compromised by agreeing to use only humanely raised, hormone-free meats.

On a strict budget, we slept in the van and used the little spending money we had to dine our way across the country. In New Orleans Ben ate crawfish while I had macaroni and cheese. In Texas he had ribs. (There being no vegetarian alternative for ribs, I didn't eat at all but just watched with a disgusted look on my face, which, to my annoyance, did not interrupt Ben's enjoyment.) In New Mexico we ate sopaipillas, and in Boulder, Moroccan tangine.

In Western Colorado, in my mother's garden—after a morning of foraging for wild asparagus—Ben sank to his knee and asked me to marry him. I delightfully accepted both the small diamond ring and the sexy man who cooked like a magician who came with it.

In Utah, we ate cherries from my grandfather's trees and green Jell-O with pineapple and marshmallows from my grandmother's kitchen, and I dared Ben to give up meat just until San Francisco. He quit cold-tofu. In protest, his system produced copious amounts of gas that permeated the van, clinging to our bedding and clothes. "It's a pre-marital test," Ben said. "If you can handle it, our marriage will be just great." He grinned, inhaling deeply, "Mmmm, essence of Ben."

Nevada offered nothing interesting to eat, do, or see. Previous travelers, in attempts to amuse themselves, had arranged words in white rocks along the roadside: "Shane and Jane forever," "Elvis is king," "Nevada sucks." Keeping the windows closed to avoid letting the hot air in, I stewed in Ben's farts, read the rocks, and hoped that we would soon find a home.

After dim sum in San Francisco—tofu for me, pork for Ben (we were both happy to see the end of that dare)—we meandered north on Highway 1. Unlike the Florida coast, which is covered with fancy homes and offers little public beach access, Northern California's endless miles of empty beaches belong to everyone. Hand in hand we walked along the shore, reminiscing about our first date back in Florida. Ben had taken me to see Eric Clapton's *Unplugged* concert. Afterwards, not ready to end the evening, we stayed up late talking by the swimming pool at my apartment. On a whim, he tossed me, fully clothed, into the pool. We swam and played in the water, time slipping away unnoticed until just before dawn, when we drove to the beach. We found a perch in an empty lifeguard's tower, where as the sun came up—finally—he kissed me. Now, two years later, we watched that same sun setting over the Pacific Ocean, an entire continent away from our first kiss. Even though we were sick of living in a van, hadn't found home yet, and were quickly running out of money, everything was just right.

Heading inland, three months after we had first set out, we found Ashland. Driving down a hill into the bustling small-town plaza, we looked at each other. I let out a giant breath that I hadn't known I was holding, and in unison we said, "This is it."

A town of only twenty thousand people, Ashland welcomes one hundred thousand visitors a year who come to enjoy its internationally renowned theater, film festival, and art galleries. Here, diamonds and tie-dye rub shoulders. Deer meander down Main Street. Ann Curry and Martha Stewart window shop. Helen Hunt and Morgan Spurlock talk movies. Neale Donald Walsh converses with God. A naked woman rides a bicycle through town. Ashland is all this, and she knows it.

Fully trusting our restaurant will be just as fabulous as the town, we decided to make Ashland home.

Settling into a small rental, Ben and I gratefully accepted the first jobs we could find. But the daily grind served as a constant incentive to get our restaurant, Pangea, off the ground. Within six months, we quit our jobs and found ourselves the proud owners of a lease. I was terrified. Starting a business was overwhelming. The restaurant equipment cost a small fortune; the *blender* was $900. Who knew so many establishments (the Health Department, outdoor dining, meals tax, the City of Ashland, Jackson County, the state of Oregon, the IRS, and the Oregon Liquor Control Commission) would need to be paid off just to open the doors for business?

Back in Florida I had done some waitressing, but working in a restaurant is nothing like starting one. I had no idea when or if we would make any money. There was a never-ending to-do list, and Ben and I were the entire team. With the exception of our menu, which we had refined during our travels, we figured everything else out as it came up. Having no plan, we simply tackled whatever was most demanding—from designing the logo to installing equipment—until we were too tired to do anything more. Then we drank coffee and kept going, eventually collapsing into bed, but not before setting an alarm so we could begin again just a few hours later.

Working this intensely seven days a week, we began to really piss each other off. Ben had his idea of how things needed to be done, and then there was the right way. Often the two didn't match up. We kept on like this for a couple of months before realizing that we would never really be ready to open the restaurant. So, with bills piling up, we did it anyway.

I still remember our first customer, a tall elderly gentleman with a kind smile who ordered coffee. I carefully wrote "coffee" on the ticket, rang him up, and gave him his change. Only then did I realize that the large industrial coffee machine was nothing like the coffee maker on my counter at home. I smiled at him, hoping I looked like someone who knew how to make coffee, and took a wild guess at portioning.

The rest of the day was much the same. I put back a salad order, to be told by Ben: "But we don't have any dressing."

If this had been a regular job, I would have quit right then. But when it's your own business, you can't. "Why is it on the menu if we don't have it?"

Ben shrugged. "I thought I would have time to make it."

"Make. It. Now," I said through clenched teeth.

He nodded.

Pasting yet another "I know what I'm doing, everything is just wonderful" smile on my face, I turned back to the customer. "It's almost ready," I promised him.

At the end of the day, we had a register full of cash. Lacking a record-keeping system, we stuffed the money into our pockets. I hoped it was more than whatever all of those ingredients we just used had cost us.

The good news was that we were wildly successful. The bad news was that we were completely unprepared for it. This, of course, is better than the other way around. Being our only employees, we did everything: the cooking, the bathrooms, the register, the ordering, the scrubbing, the graphic design, the marketing, the grilling, the chopping, the windows, the repairs, the customer service, the bookkeeping (by this I mean stuffing receipts into shoe boxes), the shopping, and of course the never-ending dishes.

After a few weeks of this nonstop manual labor, a regular customer introduced me to her teenage son and asked if we would hire him. Now there was a brilliant idea: hire help. Though this meant that I would have to learn to do payroll, it was preferable to doing all those dishes by ourselves. After realizing the benefits of having a single employee, I put a "Help Wanted" sign in the window. As our crew grew to twelve employees things got a whole lot easier.

Opening a restaurant may not be the best way to spend the six months before your wedding. But one thing was certain; Ben and I knew exactly what we were getting into. We trusted each other to not give up, even when functioning on no sleep, even when we were really, really mad at each other. So, when I found myself all dressed in white, surrounded by friends and family in my father's Colorado garden, I knew that marrying Ben was the right thing to do. As he slipped my great grandmother's ring onto my finger, it seemed almost too good to be true: a fairy tale dream turned reality for a girl who surely had too often tempted fate to deserve it.

With the wedding and restaurant under our belt, one last piece needed to be put into place before having children: a home of our own. After months of looking, we stumbled across a modest "for sale by owner" sign posted on a white picket fence covered in climbing pink rose bushes. The fence surrounded a small blue cottage with white trim. Standing on the covered porch with Ben, my hand in his, we watched birds play in the stone birdbath. I imagined growing fresh tomatoes for the restaurant in the half-acre yard and watching children climb the big apple trees.

I realized that I had done it. I had gotten my life together. The rebellious teen with a wild green mohawk, piercings in her nose and belly, and a chip on her shoulder was gone, replaced with a responsible adult who was ready to fulfill her lifelong dream of having a baby. The sellers accepted a full-price offer on the home, and, antique iron key in hand, we eagerly got to work baby-making.

When my cycle started for the first time after we had made the momentous decision to conceive, I didn't worry. Though I wistfully anticipated morning sickness, I woke each day feeling nothing more than anxiety because I was not nauseous. The second time my period came I started to think that something might be wrong with me. By the third time, I was convinced of it.

Wanting something small and cuddly, we adopted a cat from the pound. He had one blue eye like the sky and one eye as yellow as the sun, surrounded by white fluffy clouds of fur. I named him Sky.

Then it happened: my period failed to arrive on its expected date. The next morning I ran out to buy a pregnancy test. Sitting on the toilet, pee stick in hand, I thought back to the last time I had done this, four years earlier, when I realized I wanted to be married before getting pregnant. This time was different. This time, I eagerly anticipated seeing the two pink lines that the package promised would show up within five minutes if I really was pregnant.

Three minutes: one pink line.

Four minutes: still one line. *How is it fair that this stick knows more about my body than I do?*

Five minutes: still one line, but I kept watching, just in case. I'd wanted this my whole life. I could wait a little longer.

Six minutes: still one line. *It could just be slow.*

Seven minutes: still one line. I was desperate now.

Eight minutes: still one line. Though I was aware that I should throw the dumb stick out and do something constructive like corner Ben and demand sex, I wasn't quite ready to give up yet.

Twelve minutes: still one line. Knowing that I had taken this past reason, I threw the pee stick away, pushing it deep to the bottom of the trash.

Twenty minutes later, I fished it out, just to be sure: still one line.

The next day, my cycle mocked me with mild cramping and spotting but quickly disappeared again. I couldn't blame it. With everything going on, I wanted to disappear myself. I loved our new house, but our stuff was still in boxes. The old iron key looked romantic but functioned poorly. In between painting the walls and my shifts at the restaurant, I would sneak back to our old rental to nap while handy-people came and went in our new home, replacing windows and installing central heat and air conditioning, and Ben pulled up the dingy carpet and sanded the beautiful wood floors we found underneath.

During this time, we took a weekend trip to Los Angeles for an employee's wedding. Even there, far from the house and the restaurant, I was still tired. I slept ten-hour nights and then caught a nap midday. Anyone who has been pregnant would know why I was so tired, but I didn't have a clue. The pregnancy test had been negative, and I didn't have morning sickness. I had never imagined that being tired could be a symptom of pregnancy.

Arriving home from Los Angeles still without a period, I decided to try the second pee stick in the packet. Sitting on the toilet this time, I thought about how much I wished I were sleeping instead of sitting on a toilet peeing on a stick.

One minute later: two pink lines.

Pee stick in hand, I ran outside to Ben, who was cleaning out a freezer that, while we were gone, stopped working and started fermenting one hundred pounds of expensive, humanely raised, premium free-range chicken.

While he scrubbed, I blurted out:

"I took the test and it came out positive but it might be wrong because the other one from the same kit that I took last week turned out negative so I'm not sure which is right."

Ben, elbow-deep in bloody, rotten chicken, and possessing a male brain with its unfortunate disability of being able to focus on only one thing at a time, interpreted this as "I still don't know if I'm pregnant," which was not news to him. So he responded by grunting, Neanderthal-style.

Now, what I should have said was, "I am so excited that the pregnancy test is positive, but I don't want to get my hopes up, so please go get another test with me so we can find out." Instead I said, "*Fine, I will go find out on my own.*"

At the local market, I bought two types of pregnancy tests and a dozen things I didn't need to bury them from the curious eyes of Pangea's regular customers, who all seemed to be grocery shopping that night. By the time I arrived home, Ben had finished cleaning out the freezer and taken a much-needed shower.

Once again I sat on the toilet. Ben, perched across from me on the edge of the tub, watched. This time I took two tests at once. Both displayed two pink lines within the allotted time. *I am pregnant! A baby! I am going to have a baby!* In complete bliss, spooned in Ben's arms, his hands on my flat stomach, I fell asleep with a grin on my face, waking multiple times just for the pleasure of remembering that I'm pregnant.

3 Herstory

Though I have never given birth before, I am not afraid. I have witnessed three births, each one was midwife assisted and took place at home. The first I don't remember, as I was only four years old, but I don't doubt that the memory is in my subconscious. I am told that I ran in and out of the room with complete disregard as my brother Asa came into the world, and that my mom was patient and present to me the whole time.

I was fourteen when my youngest half-sister, Kelly, was born. Sitting on a chair at the base of the bed, with Asa and our golden retriever at my side and our baby half-sister, Sarah, asleep on my lap, I watched as my stepmother's body opened and a beautiful baby came out. Though I was glad to be included, I was absolutely certain I would never want anyone to watch "down there" when it came time for me to birth. I made a mental note to pick a better position when my time came, so as not be so open about things, literally.

During the months when Ben and I traveled the country looking for Ashland, we passed through Eugene, Oregon, just as my childhood friend Stella was in labor with her second baby, Alaya. I was blessed to be present for his peaceful crowning and delivery.

I have witnessed birth. I think I know what to expect. Besides, I'm tougher than Mom, my stepmom, and Stella. They are soft and feminine, emotional. I'm strong. I have no doubt that I can handle birth.

Ben assumes I will have a hospital birth "because that's where people have babies." Believing myself to be above Western medicine, I tell him I will give birth at home.

"It might be good to go, just in case," he suggests. But he doesn't push it. Ben isn't the sort to worry.

As the one who will go through birth, I believe it is my privilege and responsibility to choose the terms. I grew up trusting that my body was healthy and capable. I had seen many people whom Western medicine had pronounced at death's door heal themselves. I know that medical errors are a leading cause of death in the United States, making it safer to give birth or be born than to seek medical treatment. Birth is a normal bodily function and I believe those functions—whether eating, breathing, defecating, or giving birth—are best managed by the body they belong to.

Besides, hospitals are not particularly pleasant places to visit, much less to do something as intimate as giving birth in. They are full of big machines, bright lights, disease, trauma, and people in uniforms. I don't want strangers watching me give birth. My birth is to be by invitation only. In my own home I will be free to select whatever food or drink from my fridge that I desire, to play music that strikes my fancy, to sit on my couch or lie in my bed, to take a nap or walk in my yard, to answer my phone, cook a meal, or turn on my TV. I can choose between candles and electric lighting, either dim or bright. And when it is over, I will fall asleep in my very own bed.

Just like the books tell us to, Ben and I wait eight weeks to tell family and friends. This will be the first baby on both sides. Grandparents, cousins, and soon-to-be aunties and uncles are thrilled. To most of them, I simply say, "I'm pregnant." But, when it comes time to tell my mother, I choose our family's special language. "Mom," I ask, "will you come make mochi for me?"

With happy tears in her eyes, she replies, "Oh, yes! There's nothing in the world I would rather do than make mochi for you."

After interviewing every midwife in the book—this being Ashland, there are many in the book—we choose Laureen Sutton. Tall with long dark hair efficiently pulled back into a low ponytail, slender legs and a woman's hips and breasts, she is built like a model. Either she doesn't know it or it doesn't matter to her. Her clothing is functional: simple jeans, long-sleeved button-down shirts, a vest, and little jewelry—serving her equally well whether she is practicing midwifery or "breaking" wild horses, both of which she juggles along with mothering two beautiful girls. I am drawn to her strength. When I talk, she hears exactly what I say and then offers her wisdom, while leaving no doubt that I am the decision maker.

Laureen is the first healthcare provider I develop a relationship with. Having grown up in a family that considered themselves their own healthcare practitioners, I can count the number of times I've been to a doctor on one hand. Each visit was for a specific reason, such as a school check-up for sports or birth control. When I filled out forms asking who my doctor was, I wrote "none."

Not knowing what to expect, I find it quite natural that Laureen refers to me as a "client," meaning that I am using her services and under her protection. I much prefer this to the medical term "patient," which originates from the Latin *patiens*, meaning "I am suffering." (The adjectival meaning, is even more off-putting: "to undergo pains, trials, or the like, without murmuring or fretfulness; long-suffering.")

Laureen cares for around thirty clients a year. The average obstetrician delivers two hundred babies in that same time. Some people think that because obstetricians see more patients they are better qualified than midwives. But if more equaled better, classrooms would hold two hundred and fifty kids, and a special dinner out would be at McDonald's.

I know that I matter to Laureen and that I will not become lost in the shuffle. She will be with me from the moment I ask for her until it's over, regardless of how long that is or what else is happening in her life. When I look into her eyes I see patience and respect. I know I will be well cared for.

Our regular appointments take place in our own home. Laureen greets Ben and me with hugs. We drink tea and chat for a while about the weather, how I am feeling, and whatever else comes to mind. She listens intently to my descriptions of the changes my body is going through and examines my diet and exercise logs in detail.

Often, she concludes that I am not eating enough protein. Again and again she stresses the importance of exercise, since I never seem to fit it in. I tell her that I will. And I fully intend to. But exercise is not fun for me. Besides, no matter how much I exercise, I'm still going to get fat. I'm pregnant. Pregnant women are supposed to be fat.

After the exercise conversation, Laureen weighs me, takes my blood pressure, checks my urine, and, as necessary, draws vials of blood for routine tests. With few exceptions, she single-handedly does everything that would happen in a doctor's office.

Being a low-risk birth client, I decide not to get an ultrasound. Though I'm curious about the baby's sex, I'm not interested in undergoing a procedure that the FDA confusingly calls "safe" while simultaneously reporting that it may "restrict fetal growth and be associated with delayed speech in children."[1] Apparently my hesitancy is unique, as people don't inquire "if" I'm going to get an ultrasound. Instead, they ask, "Is it a boy or a girl?"

"Yes," I answer with complete confidence.

Laureen palpates my uterus to determine the baby's size and position. This takes place with me in my very own clothes on my very own couch or bed or wherever I happen to be. Sky jumps up to "help," kneading my belly with his paws next to Laureen's hands. Laureen speaks all the while: "Hi, baby. How are you today? Where are you baby? There you are. Oh, here's your heel. This is your leg. Feel here, Roanna, this is the baby's bum sticking right out."

Patiently, Laureen finds the place on my belly closest to the baby's heart to listen with a fetoscope. She carefully records its rhythm in my chart. Then, handing the fetoscope over, she waits while Ben and I strain to hear the soft "da-dum, da-dum, da-dum" far behind the loud rumblings of my belly and the throb of my own pulse. A good hour or more after her arrival, when the tea is finished and we are fully caught-up, Laureen reminds me (once again) to exercise, then hugs us both before leaving.

As my belly grows and rounds, strangers whose eyes would normally pass me without hesitation now stop to linger and greet me. They mention the weather, something I'm wearing, or make small talk, but then quickly abandon pleasantries to speak freely about pregnancy and labor. They touch my belly and guess "boy" or "girl." It's as if my belly is a marvelous attraction. I love this. I find the baby growing inside of me to be the most interesting and wondrous thing that has ever occurred. When people stop to talk and touch my belly, it's as if they agree.

Once someone gets their hands on my belly, they invariably feel free to ask questions about due date, doctors, and birth plans. When I respond that I will be having a home birth, more often than not my friend of three minutes exclaims with surprise, "You're so brave to have your baby at home." While I haven't thought of it as particularly brave—women have been doing this since the beginning of time, how hard can it be?—the more I hear it, the more I believe it. It doesn't take long to convince myself that I am braver and stronger than the 99 percent of women in the United States who choose to give birth in hospitals or birth centers.

In Laureen's prenatal classes Ben and I meet other expectant families, watch home birth videos, and go over everything we might expect, from when to call the midwife (whenever we want to and whenever something changes, regardless of the time of night) to what to expect in the case of a hospital transfer. I doodle as she goes over the hospital part; this clearly does not apply to me. There is no way I am going to the hospital.

I actually don't spend much time thinking about birth at all. For me, birth, however painful and difficult, is no more than the unfortunate means to a baby, I delight in feeling my baby kick and roll around inside my body. Like a bag of popcorn, my belly pops this way and that. Often, the baby hiccups, a rhythmic bump . . . bump . . . bump against my side. Caressing my belly, I feel little body parts just underneath my skin. I tell my baby, "I love you so much. You will never doubt that."

As we near the end of the nine excruciatingly slow months, Ben puts up decorative wallpaper edging in the baby's room. A pattern of fairies dancing on a blue background, it is appropriate for either a boy or a girl. He assembles the crib. Though I have heard of co-sleeping, I figure that is just for hippies. I am absolutely certain that Ben and I will need some private space and time just for us.

Laureen delivers and Ben cleans out the birth tub, a giant plastic thing that will be filled with warm water for me to relax in during the birth. Since Laureen is an equestrian and she is supplying the tub, it's a black livestock water trough. That's right. If a horse walks in while I'm giving birth, he will feel right at home leaning over to take a drink.

Home birthers are expected to invite other women to come support them during labor. I choose my mom; my sister, Eliza; and my friend from junior high, Stella—the one who poked holes in condoms with me and whose birth I attended while traveling. Each one arranges her life to be present for my birth.

These are women I value very much. Yet although each one considers me a close confidant, I do not share myself with them. "Your house could be burning down and your marriage falling apart and you would still say, 'I'm great,'" Stella claims. Though she voices it as a complaint, I consider it a compliment—proof that I'm strong and capable.

It's my male friends I feel most at ease with. Men are simple. Their straightforward, action-oriented language and lack of desire to wallow in feelings pleases me. There are no nuances, no reason to fear misunderstandings or hurt feelings.

It's been like this for as long as I can remember. On the day I was born, I learned that power, control, and safety belong to the masculine. It was a man who cut me from the womb. Though I cried for my mother, she didn't hold or soothe me. She wasn't allowed to. Newborns belonged in nurseries, mothers in recovery. Besides, there was a problem with her cesarean. In the days that followed there were complications and another surgery. She almost died. Of course, I didn't know that. I knew only that when I called for her, she did not respond. It was men—my father and uncle—who took me home, who cared for me.

As soon as she was able, Mom cradled me to her breast. She loved being a mother. She loved me. She cooked three full meals a day, took me on walks, threw the most fabulous tea parties for me and my stuffed animal friends: Lily the lion and bear, and tucked me in tenderly every night. If my life were a movie, those early years would flow in slow motion, everyone would be smiling, and jolly music would play in the background. But it wouldn't last. The images would grow darker and tension would build when I was nine and my parents divorced.

Theirs was a horrible battle with no middle ground. My mom, who I hadn't remembered ever seeing cry before, grew sad and tearful. It terrified me. So I did what, as a newborn, I had been programmed to do when my mother—my womb, my home—was broken. I chose to stay in my father's house instead of go with her.

Not understanding the significance of my actions or that I could not attack the person whose body created mine without wounding myself, I joined forces with my father in his battle for custody of my brother, his only son.

I helped him break into Mom's locked home so he could retrieve private custody battle documents, and I coaxed my brother, Asa, to "come live with me and Dad because it's more fun." And it was. I had a puppy and a baby half sister; I could watch as much TV as I wanted, and didn't have a bedtime. But really, I wanted him to come live with me because I was lonely.

My father, the product of a time when women were solely responsible for children, maintained a chilly, masculine distance. When my birthdays and small details went unnoticed, my heart broke.

Seeking connection, I would join my father in watching whatever he had on TV. Even gruesome movies like *Cujo* were preferable to the emptiness I felt outside of his office.

"It's not real," he would say when I voiced my fears of what unfolded on the screen. "Just detach yourself from it. Laugh at its absurdity."

This is how I learned to face fear.

Jane, my father's new bride, who had stepped seamlessly into my mom's position as macrobiotic cook and teacher at the residential center that was my home, was sweet and kind to me but she never tried to be motherly. Maybe, seeing the way I resisted my own mother, she didn't want to try to take her place. Or perhaps, at just twelve years older than me, she didn't know how.

I became a difficult child, learning to hide my unmet feelings and resulting insecurities behind an angry and defensive shell. I fooled everyone but my mother, who, because she had moved five hours away, I didn't see often. When we were together, she dared to try to enter this armor. But I could not see the place where the shell ended and I began. Every time she pulled at the armor, it was as if she was tearing me. So I made the armor tougher and stronger.

Mom, with the patience of someone who would eventually be ordained a Tibetan Buddhist monk, did not fight back but responded to my fury by expressing how it made her feel: sad. I didn't want to hurt her, but I couldn't let the armor that was holding me together crack. The only thing I could do was disengage. I took this to the extreme of not speaking to her for a year. During that year she battled not only the emotional fallout from losing me and my brother to my father's home but also the advanced cervical cancer that had suddenly appeared in her body.

I didn't understand. I hadn't been a mother. I hadn't learned to fear cancer. Somehow she overcame. She survived the loss of her children without becoming bitter or angry. And she resolved her cancer, as she had helped many others do, using only herbs and food.

Where my mother's love felt intrusive, at Dad's house, as long as I followed the extreme dietary restrictions expected of me, it didn't seem to matter much what I did. Of course, everyone wants to matter. Craving even negative attention over this nothingness, I became rebellious. When I yelled at my sixth grade teacher, causing her to cry in front of the class, I did not get into trouble. On the contrary, Dad, who seemed to consider me more of a small adult than child, defended me. When I turned thirteen, he introduced me to marijuana, explaining that I was going to try it anyway, so it would be best that I experience it with him. At the time, the drug didn't appeal to me; connecting to him did.

I morphed from a difficult child to an impossible teen, dying my hair green and piercing my own nose with a safety pin. Sneaking out at night with ease, I hung out with punks, drank, and smoked pot and cigarettes. When that didn't get much of a reaction, I ran away, spending one night outside on a friend's lawn furniture. In the cold that comes just before the sun rises, I took a razor blade to my wrists. It wasn't a "real" attempt. It didn't land me in the hospital. Forcing speech through the tightness in my throat, I tried to explain to my father: "Everything I do, I do for you."

"If pleasing me pleases you, then your actions are to please your-self," he replied.

Dad sent me to a therapist, who, after three sessions, informed me she was moving and referred me to someone else. I never followed through. Instead—the memory is tangible to me, it was a summer night much like any other and I was sobbing on the rough, off-white carpet in my room—I felt utterly alone. *No matter how badly I hurt myself, I can't make people love me.*

As painful as this was, like the dawn, it cracked the darkness of my sorrow. I did not need connection to exist. I could choose to live for myself alone. At age fifteen, one week into tenth grade, with a small stipend and my father's approval, I dropped out of school and moved out on my own.

If Mom, Eliza, and Stella knew the details of my childhood and the depths of the shame, regret, and sadness this armor of mine protects, they might understand why I hold them, and all other women, at arm's length. But they don't. And I won't resurrect those details. History can't be changed. It made me who I am today, someone who is independent and strong. A woman who isn't afraid of birth.

4 Blessing Way

Six weeks before my due date, Mom, excited about my pregnancy and her first grandchild, plans to come from Colorado to hold a "blessing way" to honor me. While I hope it is less touchy-feeling than the name implies, I go along with the plan because it comes with mochi, and I've been eagerly anticipating my mother making mochi for me since I was little girl.

Compiling a guest list is my only task. On a yellow legal pad I write "Stella." I move my hand down to the next line. Nothing happens. There is nothing to write. Stella is my only girlfriend. She lives three hours away, and though we have kept in touch, it's been eight years since we've spoken to each other on a regular basis. I have female acquaintances, women who I smile at and half-hug upon greeting, women who I make small talk with and whose names I know, but none who I have invited to my home or shared a meal with. For the first time in my life this bothers me greatly if only because I'm supposed to invite only female guests to the blessing way.

After much deliberation, I choose eight women who I wouldn't mind getting to know better. On the morning of the blessing way, I clean and re-clean my home in preparation for these visitors. My inclination is to wait on them. Apparently that's not what blessing ways are about. Instead, my guests begin by washing and rubbing my swollen feet in a bath of warm lavender water and floating rose petals. *Why didn't I remember to clean my toenails? . . . Oh right, because I can't reach them over my enormous belly.* I can think of a hundred things I would rather do than have my feet rubbed by people who are guests in my own home. I want to get up and offer them drinks. I want a drink, one to help me loosen up a bit. A margarita would be perfect.

After rubbing my feet, we form a circle to do a ceremony, which, compared to having my feet washed, now seems easy and maybe even fun.

"We will begin by invoking our mothers' lineages into the circle," says Stella, who is leading the ceremony. "We will each state our name, our mother's name, her mother's name, and so on, as far back as we know. In this patriarchal society, we are more familiar with our father's lineage. Although genetically, we are the result of equal parts of both our parents, on a deeper level there is a profound difference. A man's sperm constantly replenishes itself, its life cycle played out over mere months. In contrast, the egg that became you was formed while your mother was still in utero. As such, this baby she says, touching my belly, "began in her Ani's womb."

My mother, delighting in her contribution to my pregnancy, beams from ear to ear. I smile at her, knowing that she cherished and grew both me and the egg that became my baby with love.

"We each received nourishment from our grandmother's body," Stella continues. "Her joy and pain are the building blocks of our very beings."

I begin. "I am Roanna Rosewood, daughter of Ani Nyma, daughter of Verna Theurer. . . ." It is because of Grandma Verna that my list goes on. She's the one who wrote down our ancestors' names, who typed their stories and compiled them into a book. ". . . daughter of Arverna Grant, daughter of Annie Mariah Hunsaker. . . ." As I speak their names aloud, I find myself trying to imagine them joining me here in this circle. ". . . daughter of Katherine Jensen, daughter of Annie Mariah Clawsen, daughter of Anne Catherine Urbanson."

I realize that together these women formed my body. I start to wonder who they were and what brought them laughter and tears, what they wished for when they thought of their descendents, of me.

Silently, so nobody else knows that I'm feeling a bit mushy, I bless them and ask that they bless my child. I am no longer one person. I am a thread in the fabric of time, joining my ancestors in weaving the future.

Each woman takes a turn reading a blessing or poem about birth. As they speak, a red ball of yarn is passed around, each of us wrapping it once around our wrist. It forms a tangible circle, connecting us together. The linking yarn is then cut. We tie individual pieces around our wrists, a soft red bracelet to be worn as a reminder until news of birth arrives. Before closing the circle, the women give me candles to light during labor. I realize that I'm grateful they are here.

Though I enjoyed the circle more than I expected, I'm relieved that it's over. Now it's time to make mochi the old-fashioned way, the way I had seen my mother make it for other pregnant women—the way, as a young girl, I had dreamed she would make it for me someday.

Taking turns, each woman, sitting on the ground, envelopes the blue enamel pot of cooked sweet rice with her crossed legs. Grabbing both pot handles tightly, she does her best to wrestle it still while another woman, using a baseball bat, pounds the rice until every little grain bursts, mixing with the others to become one stretchy gumlike, mass. As the bat rises and falls, the entire pot attempts to follow. It's a lot of work for one pot of mochi.

With dampened fingers, we pull off small pieces of mochi, form them into balls, and roll the balls in ground walnuts to prevent them from sticking, like Crazy Glue, to everything they touch. Some mochi balls make it to the serving plate, but many more disappear into eager mouths along the way.

While it is true that a good electric mixer produces the same result, it somehow isn't the same treat. But even an electric mixer is a huge improvement over the dense, cardboard-like stuff that's labeled "mochi" and sold in health food stores.

When the women leave, I sit with a plate of mochi balls and re-read the cards and poetry they gave me. Their messages—one of my few connections to the world of women and birth—are easier to absorb now that I'm alone. I stand the candles they brought into a bowl of sand, placing it on my dresser where they will light the room during labor. The cards and poetry, I arrange alongside of them. It looks like an altar. *After the initiation of birth, will I feel comfortable in the world of women?*

Mochi
Makes about 2 cups, or 15 balls

2 cups sweet brown rice
¼ tsp sea salt
½ cup toasted chopped nuts or seeds

Soak rice for 6–10 hours. Drain and discard soaking water. Rinse. Add fresh water to cover. Bring to a boil. When boiling, lower heat, cover, and simmer for 50 minutes. Remove from heat and allow to rest for 10 minutes. Add salt.

Place rice in a heavy-duty electric mixer and knead for 10 minutes or until 90% of the grains are broken open and the mixture is sticky and smooth. Alternately, using a large wooden pestle (or baseball bat), vigorously pound the rice for 20 minutes or until the grains are broken and the rice becomes sticky and smooth.

Roll mochi into small balls about the size of a walnut shell. Then roll the balls in the toasted nuts or seeds and serve.

5 My Sun

A week before my due date, my sister, Eliza, and Mom arrive. We are now four in our small two-bedroom, one-bath home; five if we count the baby in my belly. Since I need to pee every twenty minutes, the bathroom is always in use.

The excitement is palpable; relatives from around the country start calling just to "check in." We pass our time cooking together, feeling the baby kick, visiting, and waiting.

As the due date comes and passes, the calls increase and become dominated by questions: "Is anything happening?" "How do you feel?" and the one that drives me batty: "What does the doctor say?" This last is from people who are either in denial that I'm using a midwife or feel that her opinion couldn't possibly be relevant. I find the constant inquiry annoying, even invasive. Everyone is focused on me and what my body is not doing. Mom and Eliza watch my every move during the day. Sleep would be a welcome respite, except that I wake every couple of hours to pee and remember that nothing is happening.

Fleeing the house, my phone, and my ever-watchful mother and sister, I take a walk through Ashland's beautiful Lithia Park. But there strangers join the conspiracy. "Are you carrying twins?" they ask. "You look ready to pop!" At two hundred and five pounds, I feel ready to pop. I am a pressure cooker ready to blow, a star going nova, a duck destined to become foi gras.

One week after my due date, I start to think the baby will never be born. Eliza takes the edge off her stress by nit-picking my mother, who takes this as an opportunity for all of us to express our feelings and make sure everyone is "heard." This leads to processing past issues I thought were long forgotten.

The phone calls become more demanding. "When are you going to induce?" "It's not safe to go too far past term." "My friend's cousin's husband's daughter knew someone who went too long and. . . ." I feel like I'm in a backwards IMAX movie. Instead of me watching the movie, the movie is watching me.

Days drag by. I'm too big to work in the restaurant and don't want to go out anyway. If one more person tells me I look "really pregnant," I will surely say something that a forty-one-weeks pregnant woman who is a business owner and upstanding member of the community should not say.

So I stay home. I futz with office work, reluctantly allowing Mom to drag my enormous self out for short walks every day. I hate the walks. For one thing, I constantly need to pee. For another, I don't seem able to go more than fifty feet without having to stop to catch my breath. It is during one of these walks that my first "should have" glimmers. *I should have listened to Laureen and exercised more.*

Two weeks after the due date, there are still no signs of labor. (Neither eggplant parmesan or spicy foods induce labor by the way. This I now know.) I decide that I'm not really pregnant, just really fat. Not wanting to answer anyone's questions or hear one more bit of unsolicited advice, I stop answering the phone.

My mom and sister, still processing their feelings, head to the coast, giving me a much-needed break. This must be exactly what the baby was waiting for, because the very night they leave, June 11, in the early morning hours, just as I am climbing back into bed after one of many bathroom trips, I feel a "ping" and "whoosh" as water gushes through my legs.

"My water broke," I yell, poking Ben with my finger.

"Huh?" Ben replies, squirming out of reach.

"Towels. Laureen. BEN!"

He jumps up, running to bring me towels and the phone.

"Congratulations," she says. "Now get some sleep so you will have energy to birth your baby tomorrow."

Sleep. Yeah, right. I'm going to be a mother.

Ben drifts off with no problem. I lie still, a pile of towels molded into a sort of diaper around me, caressing my belly. One tiny inch underneath my fingers is an entire person waiting to be born through me. I don't sleep but force myself to wait for the sun to lift before calling Mom and Eliza, who rush back from the coast.

Stella, three hours' north in Eugene, arranges care for her two young boys and heads down to Ashland. Laureen clears her calendar. Ben cancels his shifts at work. Together we tidy the house and spread out the birth supplies. Everything is ready. Everyone is ready. Everyone but me. There are still no contractions.

We wait.

Nothing.

Mom, Eliza, and Stella enter quietly so as not to disturb the labor I'm not having. They sit around the house making small talk, their eyes glancing at me every few moments, searching for signs of labor.

Laureen arrives to help speed things up. First on the list: castor oil with orange juice. "Repulsive" does not begin to do justice to this combination of flavor and texture. Without affecting my uterus, it quickly comes out the other end looking much the same as it did when it went in.

We try homeopathic remedies, acupuncture, and herbs. Nothing changes. Laureen sends me out for a brisk walk, which brings up mild contractions, but since I never got around to exercising during my pregnancy, I can't walk far without needing to stop to catch my breath. When I stop, the contractions stop.

By the end of the day I am exhausted and want nothing more than to sleep.

"Try stimulating your nipples," Laureen instructs on her way out the door.

"Huh?"

"Yes, stimulating your nipples can cause contractions," she says.

"Like a make-out session?" Ben asks hopefully.

"Yes. Or rub, suckle, or pull them to simulate nursing."

I frown at Laureen, hoping she is joking. She is not.

Ben, grinning broadly, says, "Don't worry Laureen. I'll take care of that."

As we lie in bed together Ben caresses my breasts. It does not stimulate me in the slightest. Instead, my mind wanders, reviewing the day and thinking of the labor I'm not in. Ben, disappointed at my lack of response, quickly loses interest and falls asleep. Picking up where he left off, I rub and pull my nipples, hoping labor will start while I sleep.

It does not.

The next day, June 12th: More castor oil, remedies, walking, acupuncture, and herbs, but no contractions. Sitting on the couch, one melon-sized breast in each hand, I rub and pull my nipples as Ben, Mom, Eliza, Stella, and Laureen watch me and wait for contractions.

Phone calls from the outer world have stopped. People are afraid to call. My frustration, palpable now, leaps through the phone lines and bites anyone who thinks of trying.

The third day, June 13th: More castor oil, remedies, acupuncture, herbs, waiting, walking, and nipple stimulation. While there are still no signs of labor, something important has changed: the rules. After three days with my membranes ruptured, infection becomes a concern. Laureen is unwilling to continue waiting for labor without a physician's blessing. This seems harmless to me, so we head to the hospital and explain the situation to the doctor. I assume he will do the necessary tests to be sure everything is safe and, providing it is, send us on our way.

Finding no signs of infection, the on-call doctor says, "We need to order an ultrasound to determine if there is enough fluid left to continue."

This sounds logical to me, so I agree.

If only I had asked, "How will the results affect recommended treatment?" The doctor would have said, "They won't. Either way, because your waters have been ruptured for so long, we will want to induce," and I could have skipped the uninsured ultrasound and would be hundreds of dollars richer today.

Sure enough, the ultrasound determines that I have plenty of fluid, and an enormous *10–11 pound baby!* (Laureen's palpations had suggested 7–8 pounds.) The doctor wants to induce. Cytotec (Misoprostol) is their drug of choice. The nurses explain its magic: "We apply Cytotec directly to your cervix, where it releases the same hormones that are in sperm, inducing labor naturally."

This gives me an idea. Having access to my own sperm-making machine, why not use the real thing? We check out of the hospital AMA (against medical advice) and head for home, where, sending everyone out of our small house, we induce by applying Ben's sperm directly to my cervix.

I should clarify right now that this was completely my idea. I did not tell my midwife about it. Though we had been encouraged to have sex before my water broke, once it did, Laureen warned us against it.

We had twenty minutes to get the job done. There was no time to set the mood. With the excitement and pressure of birth looming ahead of us, and sixty-five additional pounds of flab and fat coating my body, the situation was not conducive to good sex. In fact, it was *the worst* sex I have ever had. I did not want, get, or give foreplay, kissing, or petting. I wanted the sperm. Though the pressure was great, Ben rose to the occasion and delivered the goods.

Ben's magical and magnificent sperm works! Just after midnight, the morning of June 14th, Ben, Stella, Eliza, and I head back to the hospital with me in labor. We bring with us a small bundle of baby clothing, loads of juice, and the candles from the blessing way. My mother and Laureen, more practiced in the art of patience, go to bed, promising to come when things get moving.

At the hospital I am assigned to a new obstetrician, Dr. Carver, a short woman with brown curly hair. She talks with a slight lisp, reminding me of Elmer Fudd, except not nearly as attractive. There is no warmth in her eyes. My entourage and I are unlike her other patients. Distaste seeps from her pores. When she comes near, I force my body to not shrink from her. Thankfully, she keeps her distance, touching me as little as possible.

Ben falls asleep easily in the hospital room. Grateful to finally be in labor and afraid of losing my contractions, I do not allow myself to join him. Another dumb choice. Instead, I stoke the contractions by walking around the hospital with Eliza and Stella, who practices her newfound midwifery skills by coaching me through my breathing. They take turns leaning forward with their hands braced on their thighs, their bodies becoming soft supports for me to rest my weight on through each contraction. Through the night, the contractions slowly but steadily increase. I handle them well and feel good about my progress.

With dawn, the fluorescent lights come on, and the halls fill with people. Seeking privacy and calm, I retreat to my own room, where I pace between contractions. The nurses, having ignored me all night, increase their presence. The uniforms keep coming and going, all of them busy, none of them looking in my eyes. They want to monitor the baby's heart tones. The easiest way is to strap an electronic fetal monitor around my belly, requiring me to lie still. The strap makes each contraction more painful. Lying still makes it worse. Eventually I refuse the monitor, forcing the nurses (who exhale loudly to express their displeasure) to manually check for heart tones with a handheld Doppler.

As labor progresses and the contractions intensify, my mind slips away to laborland. I find myself unable to think clearly or articulate. It's as if the left side of my brain, the side responsible for logic, linear thought, math, consequences, routine behaviors, and linguistics, has shut off. My right brain, the instinctual and emotional side I've long refused to acknowledge, takes over.[1] Entirely consumed with the experience my body is going through, my thoughts are miles away and under water. Other people's words float slowly around, some reaching me many moments after being spoken, others drifting off unreceived. In this way, I am alone in my own body.

My support team changes. Stella and Eliza rest while Ben and Laureen coach me through the contractions. Ben holds his arms forward in front of him like two giant hooks for me to lean my full body weight on during contractions. His physical support is great. But he keeps saying "Don't worry. I've got you. I've got you. I've got you" each time a contraction pulls me under.

This I find annoying, and as soon as the contraction ends I tell him to stop. He says he will but during the next contraction, he again says, "I've got you, I've got you, I've got you." He is talking more to himself than to me. But regardless, he needs to stop. Talking during contractions is a horrible thing to do to a woman in labor. I do my best to block the "I've got you, I've got you, I've got you" from my mind until the contraction ends. When it does, I snarl "Shut up."

Ben, having said "I've got you" through the entire contraction and holding and loving me the whole time without complaint, thought he was doing a good job. Now he's being yelled at. Our timelines are off.

During labor, every thought, every movement, and every word revolves around contractions. Anything that falls out of synch with this inner dance causes excruciating pain. With so little time between contractions, time that must be used to breathe and gather myself, I am in no state of mind to explain this, so I just yell "Shut up" after each contraction.

Later Ben will explain that he said "Don't worry, I've got you, I've got you, I've got you" out of his own necessity, just as the little engine said "I think I can, I think I can, I think I can" to get up the hill. "I decided it was better to annoy you than drop you," he will tell me.

In this way we pass the day. Laureen and Mom try coaxing me to drink juice or eat something. I refuse. The thought of juice or food makes me nauseous. I accept only water and, at one point, some soup broth.

Knowing the labor dance well, Laureen speaks only between contractions and limits her words to direct instructions, quietly showing me the most effective positions. In this way we work with the contractions, willing my body to open. When the nurses or doctor come to check on me, Laureen retreats to a corner, observing quietly. This is their territory. She concedes to their power.

Eventually Ben learns to shut up and once he does, goes from annoying to amazing. He is completely present, working with me, holding me up through each contraction. He is quiet and still when I need him to be. Only when he can see that I want language does he whisper that I am doing a good job. His eyes, his gorgeous blue eyes, become the lighthouse through the storm in my body. They are all I can see.

Eliza asks Dr. Carver if we can bring in a birth tub. Miraculously, she agrees. I bet she expected something pink and soft.

Laureen and Eliza bring the giant black livestock water trough to the hospital, strapping it upside down on top of Laureen's old Subaru station wagon. Together they carry it through the waiting area, down the hall, and into the room.

They fill the tub with warm water, turn off the fluorescents, and light the candles. I get into the fabulous, warm tub and release into the water. Laureen stays with me, showing me how to squat down into the contractions to encourage my cervix to open. Things begin clicking into place. Though I haven't slept or eaten in thirty-six hours, my resolve is strong. I work at it with everything I have and am rewarded with intensifying contractions. By 8:00 pm, I have dilated to 7–8 centimeters. Contractions are now a steady three minutes apart.

Dr. Carver comes in to check on me. This is not fun for her. She is used to having her patients on beds, strapped up to fetal monitors, all neat and orderly and easy for her to examine. Though she had agreed to a bath, this is not what she expected.

"Candles are a fire hazard. Put them out. You are running out of time," she says.

Dr. Carver's words—her very presence—disturb me. In hindsight, I should have asked for a different doctor, but I did not know that labor would be so big and intimate, that trust and comfort would be essential to progress. As an articulate person, I had assumed I would be able to rationalize through labor, to troubleshoot, to concentrate and verbalize and make decisions. I was wrong.

Every time Dr. Carver comes in the room, I sense her disapproval and dislike. My body responds accordingly. Instead of working with the contractions, pushing myself to go deeper into the intimacy of birth, part of me resists in an attempt to "pull myself together" while the doctor is in the room. Though the pain and intensity do not diminish, the contractions slow. While before they followed one on top of another, now there is a brief stillness between each one—not enough to rest or collect myself, only enough for my mind to taste the fear of anticipation of the next contraction. It's not a conscious response. My body and mind are no longer under my control.

By 1:00 am on June 15th, dilation has not changed in five hours. I've not slept for two nights. I am tired and scared. There is no end in sight.

Given no alternative, I agree to Pitocin. They do not tell me it requires wearing the electronic fetal monitor and my lying still in a prone position. Now gravity works against me. Being on my back closes my pelvis 30 percent, putting bones and cartilage in front of what was a pretty small opening to begin with. My body now battles itself.

The Pitocin changes the pain. Before it was purposeful, telling my body how to move and what to do; now it's just pain. If someone were to offer an epidural I would accept, but the words to ask for it are lost to me. Nurses and the doctor come and go: a rotating merry-go-round of uniforms. I cannot remember what it was like before this suffering or believe it will end. Nothing outside of the sensations happening to my body seems real—everything, everyone else is a dream. My mind whimpers one repetitive thought: *Please no. Please no. Please no. . . .*

Hours later, the Pitocin has not worked. The uniforms say something about the baby's heart. They are worried about the baby's heart. Somewhere there are questions I would ask—if I could just remember what they were, if I could remember how to form words. I am swimming in pain, the words "cesarean" and "distress" floating alongside me. I don't want my baby to die. I don't know what to do. The only option given is a cesarean.

I nod.

Now that it's been decided, the uniforms leave, giving me the peace and quiet I had been craving. Ben cries. I do not. I am empty, wrung dry. Continuing contractions mock me. I want it over. I want the pain to go away. *They said the baby is in distress. What are they waiting for?* Now that we have agreed to a cesarean, the uniformed ones seem to have all the time in the world. *They said my baby is in danger. Why aren't they doing anything?*

An hour and fifteen minutes later, they return, having multiplied into many masked and capped people. They wheel me into a cold room where I am told to sit up and hold perfectly still. The stillness hurts such that I do not feel the needle go into my spine, only its effect: numbness and relief. I am no longer in the body that these things are happening to. I hover around it, not sure what else to do.

It is bright. The uniformed ones talk about the weather. Another day. Another job. Co-workers visiting around the water cooler, except that I am the water cooler: bloated, freezing, immobile, and speechless. My arms are strapped down. Drugs render all movement but the rolling in my stomach impossible. I think about death—not in a fearful way but a resigned one. I might die. I don't care. I ... am ... so ... tired.

They are cutting flesh. The machines make slurping and whirring noises. There is pulling, yanking hard, and pressure in the chest of the body that I used to be inside of. It can't breathe. The pulling, they are pulling the insides of the body out, cutting and yanking. There is classical music playing. The body vomits, thin greenish fluid dripping down the side of its cheek. Its cuffed hand cannot wipe it away.

Ben's blue eyes hold me, stopping me from floating away from the body that used to be mine.

At 5:04 am, I hear my baby's cry. I am a mother. I have a baby. "It's a boy," they say, lifting him in front of my eyes. I see an exquisite face covered in white vernix and blood with a head full of black hair. He is big and beautiful and he is my son. In a blink, he is gone. They take him ten feet to my right. He is screaming with all of his might. I strain to see him but cannot. He is surrounded by uniformed ones.

Why don't they give him to me? What is wrong? Every instinct in my body demands that I get up and go to him. I can't. I'm tied down. My womb is sitting outside of my body. Drying vomit tickles my cheek.

They continue working on me, removing the placenta, throwing it and the cord away: pieces of me I had planned to bury in the ground and plant a tree over. It doesn't matter now. My baby needs help. *Can't they hear him calling me? Please help my baby.* Oblivious, to his loud wails and my silent prayers, they blather on: "Very vigorous, Apgar nine,★ seven pounds, eleven ounces. . . ."

Nine is a good Apgar. Why are they ignoring his screams? Why won't they give him to me?

Leaving me, Ben goes to our baby. Papa speaks. Our son stops screaming, recognizing his father's voice from the beginning of time. It is the only familiar element in this new, loud, bright, and waterless world. They look into each other's eyes, seeing each other for the first time. I am relieved that my baby is comforted. I am a mom, but not really. It's Ben he sees, Ben he bonds with. I watch Ben's back.

When the uniforms finally finish with my son, Ben carries him to me. He is fresh and clean. All traces of birth—all traces of me—have been wiped from his body. He is beautiful: a present all wrapped up with a cotton cap covering his thick black hair. *Or did I just imagine hair?* Ben sits next to me, holding him. A uniform releases one of my arms from its cuff. I start to reach out and touch my baby—but my arm won't work. The drugs have rendered my hand too heavy to lift. I watch Ben caress him.

Later, in recovery, the room is dimly lit and warm. The white gowns finally leave. I lie motionless, my arms still unresponsive. Unable to hold my baby, my body shaking uncontrollably, I succumb to sleep. Mom and Laureen help my baby nurse. They hold him in position close to my heart, using my body to provide nourishment to my son, connecting him to what is left of me.

Hours later, I awake and fall in love with this beautiful boy, completely in love. He sleeps next to me in the hospital bed, nursing

---

★ An Apgar score is a test used to quickly assess the health of a newborn directly after birth. Any score over 7 is considered normal, with 10 being the highest.

greedily when I wake him. Taking the cap off of his head, I uncover the full head of hair I wondered if I had imagined. I inhale him deeply, delighting in his toes, the softness of his cheeks, and the noises he makes as he latches onto my breast.

He is everything I wanted. He is perfect—me, not so much. I didn't know how important my belly is to every movement. The electric hospital bed is the only way I can lift my body into a sitting position. When I cough or sneeze, it feels like the incision is ripping open. Laughter would have the same affect, but I don't feel like laughing.

If something is not located on the near edge of the side table, I cannot reach it. When his diaper needs changing, I must ask others to do it. When he needs a bath, I watch wistfully from the hospital bed, imagining that it's my hands tenderly holding his precious head up from the water. I am grateful to everyone for caring for us, for delivering me a perfect baby, for doing all of the things mothers should be able to do but I cannot. To thank them, I order a big dessert tray from Pangea for the hospital staff.

The first time my fingers venture under the bandage, I notice that although they feel my belly, my belly does not feel them. There is no sensation. It's as if I am touching someone else, someone who is cold, as cold as an operating room. Bracing myself, I hold my breath to look. I had expected stitches, but they used large construction-type staples. The cut is long across my lower belly. It looks haphazard. The right side is twice as thick and half an inch lower than the left. Badly swollen, the incision oozes blood and clear liquid. Where the skin meets in the middle, it is dry and crispy. A piece breaks off when I touch it. I cannot tell where my living body ends and the dead begins. My belly, once bursting with life, repulses me. Moving my hands away, I take care not to touch or think about myself more than I have to.

Instead, I spend my hours staring into my son's eyes, drinking him in. I'm convinced that this nursing, pooping, burping, crying, fabulous baby is the most beautiful baby in the world. He is my light in the dark: my sun: my son.

6 Nummie Woman

When I check out of the hospital three days after the surgery, my body is a disgusting prison. I'm swollen and bloated and weigh more than when I checked in still pregnant. Arriving home, I remember the naïve girl who had walked out of this house just a few short days earlier, the one who considered herself superior to hospitals and pain medications—a stark contrast to the person I have been reduced to, a woman who cannot birth at all. Not at home. Not in the hospital. Not with Pitocin. I didn't birth my son. They cut him from me, handing him to me like a gift.

As if to prove I am worthy, I push myself, taking as few pain meds as possible. I need to be in control again. Using nothing but my arms and will (my abdominal muscles still don't function), I force myself out of bed and use the "ceasarean shuffle" (feet flat, knees unbent, minuscule "steps") to get around. I carry the baby in a bright rainbow-colored Mayan sling while cooking, working on the computer, tidying the house, and making tea for visitors.

Mom tries to make me stay in bed to rest and recover. But I refuse. Bed does not bring peace. It reminds me of the cesarean. Dreams of being tied down and cut open haunt my nights. I spend my days relentlessly proving that even though I couldn't birth, I deserve this baby.

We name him Avram, a variation of Abraham, meaning "father of nations." It's a big name for such a small person, but it suits him.

Determined that Avram will sleep in a crib in his own room, we take turns sitting up late rocking, walking, patting, and singing him to sleep. But he is a determined bugger. Knowing we will walk out once he closes his eyes, he fights sleep with the will of a babe who, having known only the warmth of his mother's womb and sound of his parents voices, believes with his whole heart that being close to them is his birthright.

When he does fall sleep, we have to close the door so Sky Kitty, who wants to be next to him, can't get in. Sky's body is significantly larger than Avram's small swaddled one, and Sky is so enamored with him that I once caught him lying on Avram's face.

I don't like having a closed door between us. I want to be able to check on him—to make sure his breath still rises and falls steadily, to replace the soft, fuzzy cloud-covered blanket if it slides off of him—without the creak the door makes waking him. Even with the baby monitor, I worry that I won't wake when he calls me to nurse, as he does two or three times a night.

I don't mind waking to nurse him. It's keeping awake that's difficult. One night, I accidentally drift back to sleep all curled up with the sweetness that is Avram. When, hours later, I stir to realize that he has latched on for his next nursing and I can fall back to sleep without having to venture out from the warmth of my bed, the solution is obvious: we all get more sleep if we skip the negotiations and begin the night with Avram nestled in the crook of my arm. He is going to end up there anyway. Now if I wake in the middle of the night, it's only to press my nose into his neck to smell his soft breath and give thanks for him.

My favorite part of sleeping together is waking up in the morning to re-discover that this beautiful boy is my son. If I wake before he does, I nuzzle and kiss him until he yawns and stretches, opening his eyes to see me. In this way, without leaving our cozy bed, Ben, Avram, and I start every day connecting and enjoying the gift of each other: one big puddle of family.

Sleeping with Avram doesn't make me nervous; I would sooner roll off the bed and onto the floor than roll over my baby. My in-laws, however, are horrified. "He won't ever leave. He will sleep in your bed forever. You're going to regret it."

This worries me a little, but the need for sleep seems more important than concerns about the distant future. And their alternative of letting him "cry it out" is unbearable to me.

As it turns out, I will never regret this decision. By the time Avram is ten and too cool to be seen hugging me good-bye, I will be grateful for the nights when his friends aren't around and he invites me to hold him as long as I want. No matter how mad he will make me, or how many times I will tell him to pick up his room, eat neatly, or do his homework, when I climb into bed, rearranging his long arms and legs to make room for myself, I will brush the hair from his sleeping eyes, kiss his dirt-smeared cheek, and give thanks for the wonderful person that is my son.

Ben is a magnificent papa. Somehow, I had thought that dads only helped when asked. But Ben adores Avram as much as I do. He changes diapers, pats him to sleep, and holds him just for his own pleasure.

I finally have the baby I wanted my whole life. He is beautiful and healthy. I'm happily married with a successful business and a house with a white picket fence. Everything is better than I could have imagined—everything but me.

In the quietest part of the night, when Ben's breathing is steady and deep and Avram's soft lips have released their seal on my breast, when I am alone with myself, tears flow. It's the cesarean. Flashes of it do not stop coming. *Why can't I let it go? Why do I cry when the end result is exactly what I wanted: a beautiful, healthy boy of my own?*

What I expected to be easy instead left my body broken. But that's not what wakes me in tears. The memory of failing Avram does. His perfect ears were formed inside of my body while listening to my promise that he would never doubt my love, that no matter what, I would be there for him. It was a lie. Even before he experienced my touch, he was stolen from the dark warmth of my womb. The gloved hands and masked faces of strangers pulled him into freezing air, suctioned his nose, and wiped his body with paper towels as he took his first breath. They took prints of his feet, tagged his wrist, clamped an alarm to his umbilical cord, and measured him.

Why must a baby be measured immediately at birth? How much can he grow in an hour?

They did a thousand little meaningless things while, with all his might, he asked for one thing: me, his home, his mother. Avram's first experience was of being abandoned. He doesn't understand that I couldn't go to him, that I wanted to more than I had ever wanted anything, and that I would have paid any price just to fulfill my promise.

Why couldn't the procedures have waited for just a few minutes so he could first experience the world from the warmth my bare chest, complete with soft kisses and the familiar sound of my heartbeat? Footprints taken at ten minutes old surely look the same as those taken immediately after delivery, but a baby's first experience of the world only occurs once. Avram wanted me. I was not there. It's not what they did to me that haunts me, it's what I didn't do for my son.

Trying to understand what happened, I research cesareans, learning that even though the World Health Organization says "there is no justification for any region to have a [cesarean] rate higher than 10–15 percent," [1] the hospital I was in has a rate of over 25 percent.

Was my cesarean necessary? I don't want to consider that it might not have been. I don't want to believe that maybe I could have tried harder. Just because the hospital I birthed at has a cesarean rate twice as high as it should be does not mean my cesarean was unnecessary. *Or does it? Were the doctors heroes who saved my baby, or were they just tired of dealing with me and anxious to go home?*

I remember how their fancy ultrasound machine said that Avram weighed 10–11 pounds and was "too big" for me to birth vaginally. In contrast, Laureen's patient and soft hands had judged him to be 7 1/2 pounds, an almost exact match to his birth weight of 7 pounds 11 ounces. How is it that a cutting-edge, costly test can be so off when a midwife's opinion, widely considered secondary to a doctor's, nails it? And shouldn't I get a refund because their stupid test was wrong? At Pangea, if the food doesn't come out like the menu says, we refund the customer's money and apologize. This is customer service 101.

The more I learn, the more whatever faith I had in the system dissolves. Basic birth books—*why didn't I read these before labor?*—clearly say that lying on one's back can cause the baby's heartbeat to show distress. I remember how much I hated every moment of lying on my back, how painful it was and how the nurses had refused to allow me to move. Though I spent only a couple of hours in this position, these hours just happened to be when the monitor showed fetal distress, which was why I "needed" a cesarean. The nurses were so busy measuring Avram's heartbeat, they didn't allow me the freedom of movement that might have improved it.

I see how this could have been an oversight: a dumb one, but innocent. It's what I learn about Cytotec, the drug that they wanted to use to induce labor before I extracted Ben's Magnificent Sperm, that convinces me it was more than oversight. There is something seriously wrong with our maternity care system. They told me Cytotec was "natural and safe" and I thank God, or fate, or even my own anti-Western medicine upbringing that I did not take that horrible drug.

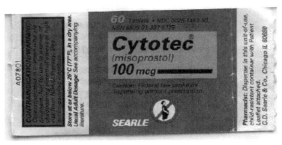

Cytotec is an ulcer treatment drug. Not only has it not been approved by the FDA for women in labor; it is specifically contra-indicated by the FDA, the World Health Organization, Searle (the manufacturer of Cy-totec), and many other

Label Reads:
CONTRAINDICATION/WARNING:
Contraindicated in women of childbearing potential unless at high risk of NSAID therapy.

gynecologist and obstetrician groups around the world.[2] A bright red warning on the label says it is not for use by women who are pregnant.

Just in case the person handling the drug doesn't read or speak English, the label includes a visual: a pregnant woman inside a circle with line through it.

The devastating stories of pain, torn uteruses, hysterectomies, and mother and baby deaths attributed to this drug shock me. The doctor and the nurses hid this from me. I'm sure that if I were to confront them with this information, they would tell me, quite truthfully, about the numerous times they have used it without problem, and how hospitals all over the country use it regularly. But this rationalization is wrong. With risks of this magnitude, the only person who has the right to overrule such a warning is the one who must live with the outcome for the rest of her life. Mothers must be given the right of informed consent.

Cesareans are also dangerous.[3] Complications may include: cutting of the baby, respiratory problems, celiac disease, hemorrhage, infection, depression, chronic pain, bowel obstruction, and PTSD.

Who do cesareans benefit? As a business person, I know the answer. A cesarean takes 88 percent less time to perform than a vaginal birth while producing almost twice the revenue.[4] If I could cut my employees' time by 88 percent while doubling my revenue, paying for this uninsured cesarean would be a piece of cake—red velvet, of course. Many people—doctors, nurses, drug companies, anesthesiologists, hospital administrators, and investors—benefit from the cutting of a woman.

It's no wonder that babies, who used to arrive at all hours of the night, and on weekends and holidays also, are now most often born on weekdays.[5] The ability to schedule deliveries allows staff to get home for dinner and sleep without interruption.

Cesareans also protect against litigation.[6] A well-known saying in labor and delivery wards is "the only cesarean you are ever sued for is the one that you didn't do."

As I read about cesareans, my hands, repeating the habit they formed when I was pregnant, gravitate to my belly, only to find it numb and cold. They circle and press as if expecting it will recognize their caress and become warm once again. *Silly hands, my belly doesn't want to feel.*

My anger at Dr. Carver and the hospital deflects some of the shame and disappointment I feel about myself. *If only* becomes my constant thought. I detest it, but I cannot stop it. It echoes through my dreams: *If only I had transferred to the other hospital. If only I had induced on my own sooner. If only I had asked for a different doctor. If only I had eaten during labor. If only. . . .*

Despite the "if only's" of my dreams, my days are wonderful. Being a mom brings me even greater joy and satisfaction than I had imagined. From watching Avram discover his fingers and their ability to bring objects of desire to his mouth or splash water with them to the way he laughs and blows raspberries, I am completely in love with my son.

"Is he really beautiful?" I ask Laureen. He looks picture perfect to me, the kind of baby seen on magazine covers and in movies. I don't actually care if he's beautiful. I would love him just as much if he were ugly. I just need to know if I'm delusional. "All mothers think their babies are beautiful, even if they are ugly, right?"

"He is one the most beautiful babies I've ever seen," she tells me.

I believe her.

Like a magnet, Avram draws everyone to him. In a matter of months, my mom decides Colorado is too far away and moves to Ashland to be closer to us.

Before Avram, I paid little attention to what seemed to be the insignificant details of life. Now they are everything. Where before I would eat whatever I felt like eating whenever I was hungry, now that I am responsible for a whole other person, it seems important to make three healthy meals every day, to go outside and get fresh air, to keep the house spotless, and to wear seatbelts.

My thoughts, previously confined to what would be my own eighty some odd years on the planet, now stretch forward in fear and hope to unborn generations and back, in gratitude, to those whose sacrifices brought me here. We open retirement and college savings accounts and write wills. Recycling, donating to environmental groups, and building community suddenly matter to me.

With parenthood comes a lifetime membership to the parent's club. As part of the club, I can immediately, without needing reason, strike up a conversation with any member. "How old is your son?" "Ohhh boy, look at him crawl!" "How do you get him to eat yams? Mine doesn't like yams." It's insta-friendship. Where before I thought parents were the odd ones, now I realize that non-parents are the ones who just don't get it. They can't. There is no way to understand how all-consuming and identity-changing being a parent is without becoming one.

Invited to join a small moms' group, I find myself, for the first time in my life, spending time with a group of women. We meet once a week. While our children play together, we talk about parenting. It's fun to compare notes and to watch Avram interact with other babies.

But these women don't just talk about parenting; they also talk about womanhood and feelings. I do my best to divert the conversation back to something feeling-free: recipes, the weather, the merits versus dangers of binkies, the abundance and consistency of babies' poop—anything but feelings. Sometimes this tactic works. Other times, they smile indulgently at me and, without missing a beat, continue their conversation.

When they talk about birth, my throat swells and my eyes burn. To hide my reaction, I find things in the other room to occupy my attention. I know that each of them birthed naturally. If I told them about Avram's delivery, they would be kind and supportive. But I don't want kind and supportive. I prefer tough and unconcerned.

With this weekly women's group, most of my social time is now spent with women, but I still relate more easily to men. Had I expected having a child would change that? Maybe. Would birthing naturally have changed it? I'm not sure. Maybe it's naïve to think that something as commonplace as birth would change the true north of my compass.

Breastfeeding does soften me, though. I hadn't expected to like it at all. What could be fun about sitting around having one's breast sucked? In a word: oxytocin. It pumps through my system as Avram pumps milk from me. Ferocious at first, he works to get the milk flowing. Once it does, everything else fades away; there is only the two of us. He looks into my eyes, moaning "mmmmmm" in satisfaction. Doped with love, we are as high as two stoners on a binge, delighted to do nothing but explore each other. He ever so gently touches my face, investigating my mouth with his fingers. I caress him back, ruffling his unbelievably soft hair, watching the roundness of his cheek as it pumps my milk into his body. This is the best.

I hadn't thought much about breasts until now. They had been average-sized oranges that willingly flopped along with me without comment. Now heavy, melon-sized protrusions, each one bigger than Avram's head, they have their own agenda. To start with, they leak. I might glance down while ringing a customer up on the register to see two round wet spots on my shirt. This can sometimes be prevented by pressing hard into my nipples with my palms—a maneuver that becomes so habitual that only when I receive a strange look do I remember the grocery store isn't the best place to grope myself. And when my breasts tingle—look out, I need to nurse now! There is no stopping the tingle flow. I drop whatever I'm doing and head home to Avram, who, across town, like magic, started fussing the moment the tingling began.

Ben's parents come to visit. When my father-in-law, seated on our couch in our living room, asks of our nursing, "Can't you do that somewhere else?" I half stand to leave the group conversation and nurse in another room. But the cover of my mother-in-law's glossy fashion magazine, lying on the coffee table, offers reason to pause. A woman is on the front. Her lips pout, her eyes have a dopey expression, and her breasts are more exposed by her minimalist top than mine are while nursing. Why should the sexualized breasts displayed everywhere in this culture, from beer ads to magazine covers, be acceptable while mine, feeding my son with the best nourishment in the world, are hidden away?

Deciding that other peoples' discomfort is not my problem, I respond: "Perhaps you'd prefer to focus on the breasts in that magazine while I nurse." In my defense, I say it sweetly. In his, he leaves the room without further protest.

Until this exchange, I had never been much of an exhibitionist. Now I see that my breasts are more than entertainment for Ben; I recognize them for what they are: powerful super food makers. Where I used to modestly cover them, now, regardless of my surroundings—airport, restaurant, park, or grocery store—when Avram is hungry, I feed him openly.

Why, even though it's widely accepted that "breast is best," are bottles still the norm? Determined to normalize breastfeeding, as part of my personal protest I walk up to strangers, Avram contentedly nursing in my arms, to ask them random questions: "Excuse me, do you have the time?" "Any idea where a grocery store is?"

I watch as they struggle to contain their reaction, to not let their eyes drift to my exposed breast. I don't do it to make them uncomfortable. I do it because I want to live in a world where women and their babies are not ostracized to bathrooms to nurse every two hours.

I can nurse and knit, nurse and walk, nurse and shop. If it were safe, I could even nurse and drive. (Don't ask how I know.)

Settling into our family bed one night, Ben, whose sense of humor is questionable, looks across the bed at Avram and me, quietly nursing, and says, "You're like a built-in cow." Not wanting to disturb Avram, I lift my other "nummie" (Avram's word for both a breast and nurse) and, squeezing it gently, shoot a stream of milk at Ben, who scrambles out of bed even faster than he jumps into it when I'm naked and inviting. Avram finds this worthy of pausing his meal to grin conspiratorially at me. I grin back, my breast still cocked in Ben's direction. Sheepishly, Ben admits defeat. To signal that it's safe for him to return to bed, I let go of my nipple.

In this moment, "Nummie Woman" is born. No longer a mere mortal, I am a super hero. In addition to being able to quiet the loudest screaming baby, I can send grown men running with my enormous built-in, milk-squirting nummies. Well-primed, they can reach a good twelve feet. What they achieve in distance, however, they lack in aim, sending bystanders and foes alike ducking for cover.

In what seems like a single moment, Avram has gone from rolling over to sitting to crawling and then taking his first steps. He is a fireball, using momentum instead of balance to keep himself up. My baby is gone, replaced with a toddler. Before, I was the center of his universe. Now, he is an explorer, and I am the person who stops him from splashing in the pond and chasing the swans, from climbing out of car windows, and from eating candy off the ground. He is visibly annoyed when I limit his freedom. The look on his face is not so different from the way I felt as a teenager. Except now I'm the parent.

Avram is still only when he sleeps. This he valiantly fights off until the bitter end, rubbing his eyes with his fists until finally, his little body spent, he lies with legs splayed out, one hand on his belly, the other up and behind his head "en garde" style. His short legs are covered with typical toddler's bumps and bruises. His hair, which I haven't yet brought myself to cut, hangs down past his eyes. I hold him close and, together with Ben and Sky Kitty, we sleep.

7 Snake Oil

In the spring, almost a year after the cesarean, to all outside appearances, I have recovered, but in fact my body is not the same. Sensation never returns to my belly. A thick, cold, rubber layer seems to lie between it and my fingers. Sudden random pains in the right side of my scar cause me to double over. They feel as if the incision is tearing. Even when I'm not in pain, there is a constant nagging "something is wrong" feeling.

Flashes of the cesarean still haunt my nights, causing my eyes to flood. I am sick of this but don't know how to stop it. A simple book hands me the answer. It's a compilation of stories of women who have had a vaginal birth after cesarean (VBAC). Each story in the book opens the floodgates again. But these tears are different. I am no longer alone in my sadness. These tears are for others who, after being cut open, had beautiful natural births. Logically, I conclude that because a cesarean broke me, a "real birth" will fix me.

I harness all of the anger, tears, and shame into one sole purpose: VBAC. No longer naïve, I will be ready for the next birth. So I call Dr. Carver and ask, "What can I do to prepare for a vaginal birth?"

"You have a small pubic arch. A baby won't fit through it."

Her reply delights me because it is the same reason given to many of the women in the VBAC book who were able to birth naturally. There is nothing small about my pelvis. Long ago, before Barbie Dolls set impossible standards, I would have been complimented for my "birthin' hips."

Though undisturbed by Dr. Carver's statement, I want to do something to ready myself for natural birth. I've had enough of the tears. I want to take action. The only alternative is the alternative. I begin exploring other kinds of medicine.

I start conservatively, with a chiropractor. I tell him about the sharp recurring pains I get deep in the right side of my cesarean scar. He twists and contorts me and advises lots of walking. I walk every day, up big hills, pushing Avram ahead of me in a bright red stroller. I hate every nanosecond of it, but that is irrelevant. I don't have to like it; I just have to do it.

At Laureen's suggestion, I rub vitamin E deep into the scar and apply hot castor oil compresses. The pains in my side continue.

A physical therapist palpates and stretches my abdomen. An acupuncturist inserts needles all over my body. But the sadness inside, like a whiny child, does not stop.

Desperate to block it out, I begin going through practitioners the way Avram eats: willing to try anything, even bugs. An herbalist supplies foul-smelling herbs that I brew and drink three times a day to increase my *chi*, holding my nose while gulping down the tea in an attempt to avoid fully experiencing its wormy flavor. I try flower remedies ("essence" of flowers in brandy), finding them easy to take, with no foul side-effects. In fact, I can't perceive any effects at all.

I try a different chiropractor. This one insists I walk on flat ground instead of the steep hills surrounding my house, so I buy a treadmill and walk or run every day. A kinesiologist (muscle tester) holds vials of suspected allergens in one hand as she pushes down on my opposite arm, testing the strength of my resistance. Either she is a complete fake (sometimes pushing down hard, other times softly) or my arm muscles really do become weak just by holding different foods. I'm not surprised when she eliminates sugar, coffee, chocolate, and flour (are these good for anyone?) but there are some shockers: strawberries, canola oil (which is in almost every prepared product) pork (having never tried it, this doesn't bother me), gluten, peanuts, and tomatoes.

A second acupuncturist turns me into a pincushion. The needles do not hurt going in, but this man seems to think that tweaking each needle until it stings makes it work better. I welcome the pain. It is nothing compared to a cesarean.

I try craniosacral therapy, described as "restoring the rhythmic movement found in the bones of the skull." I expect this to mean a head massage. Instead, the therapist puts her fingertips on the end of my tail bone. This I was not expecting. She holds perfectly still. As do I. I'm not sure what is happening, and her fingers are really close to the inside of my butt. *If I move, they might slide right in.* I hold perfectly still, waiting for her to move up to my head already. She does not but instead begins to make miniscule circling movements with her fingertips. This continues without change for a good number of minutes before I realize that this is it. This is the appointment, her fingers circling around right inside the tip of my butt crack. *This is why it costs $100. Probing people's butt cracks can't be much fun.* I can sense how the spine connects to the top of my head as I drift off to sleep. Coming to forty-five minutes later, my body feels relaxed and melty, like a lovely pool of mush. While nice, in a strange, butt-cracky sort of way, this does not help the pains in my incision site at all. And I still have the irritating sense that "something is wrong."

Homeopathy is next, a centuries-old alternative medicine using tiny sugar pills infused with such low amounts of their original formulation that no molecules of that substance can be scientifically detected. My appointment begins with an interview by a short, round homeopath named Louise. The questions she asks seem ridiculous: "What body parts are cold? What ones are hot?" "What colors do you like? How do you feel when it rains? What position do you sleep in? How do you deal with stress? What does your sweat smell like?"

The questions go on for *one and a half hours.* When she is finished, Louise gives me a small, brown glass container containing a few dozen tiny round white pills. "Be careful to not touch the pills because oils or dirt from your hand will destroy the shadow of formulation," she tells me. "Take them by dropping them into spring water, *not* tap water. Then stir clockwise six times and three times in reverse."

Dumbfounded, I nod.

"Oh, and be sure you don't eat or drink anything for twenty minutes before or after taking the pills or drink coffee at all. Ever. Or use mint—even to brush your teeth."

Does it work? There's no way to find out until I have another baby, so how the frick do I know? Unwilling to depend on any modality I've tried, I seek out other practitioners.

Someone—I don't know what kind of someone you would call him—palpates my belly. He determines that nothing is wrong where I get the pains but announces: "Your liver is out of place."

I didn't know livers could fall out of place. "Can you put it back?" I ask, not sure that I want to hear the answer.

"Just hold still and breathe deeply," he says with a grin. Seemingly oblivious to my skin and whatever other tissue, bones, or cartilage is in the way, he grabs my liver and pulls and pushes until it's back to where it "belongs."

"Ow."

Though this does not improve the pains I get deep in my belly, I am pleased to report that my liver (which I had thought was fine before) is still fine after its relocation.

Jason, a short, bald man with a long goatee, uses little round magnets to "work my meridians" without needles. First he marks each magnet with a plus sign on one side and a minus sign on the other. Using a permanent marker, he marks spots on my arms, legs, belly, back, and neck with the same signs. Matching opposite signs together so that plus is next to minus, with masking tape Jason sticks a magnet to each spot. In my ears he sticks tacks (mini acupuncture needles). The magnets and tacks he covers with little squares of masking tape to hold them in place.

I leave his office with a dozen bits of masking tape polka-dotted all over my body. At home, I change into long sleeves and pants, which cover 80 percent of my tape-ridden body. These I wear all summer, diligently reapplying both the marks and the masking tape after every shower.

I try rapid eye movement therapy, which involves blinking my eyes while watching a wand move back and forth as I tell the story of Avram's delivery. I pause each time my throat tightens and tears threaten to flow. The therapist coaxes me to say now what the me in my past needed to hear. The idea is that I will reach, consciously, the same deep recesses of my mind that engage during the rapid eye movement stage of sleep, thereby connecting my right and left brains and reprogramming them to accept the past. Though the treatment does not alleviate my anger or physical pains, the nightmares become less violent.

Ben doesn't seem to mind my forays into alternative medicine. Of course, that could be because he hasn't asked how much they cost. Let's just say they are neither cheap nor covered by insurance.

By fall, I begin to run out of practitioners, but the pains in the right side of my scar continue and the pressure from my well of tears, though lessened, is still strong. There is nowhere left to turn but the seriously alternative. First I go to a re-birther who promises to "re-create and heal" my own "birth experience." I don't know what to expect, but it can't hurt to try, right? Ha. It doesn't hurt, but it does suck. I find myself lying in the fetal position on a brown matted carpet with this woman, who I had just met, *lying on top of me*. She is trying to encompass my whole body with hers, her hands pushing on my head.

"Push! Push through the birth canal. You can do it!" she encourages me.

I try to play along. I do. But I, who clam up, giving my seat a hickey, at the mere mention of birth, cannot stop laughing at the absurdity of this. Making a feeble excuse, I leave as quickly as I can.

Lastly, I engage Gwen, a medical intuitive. A large and surprisingly "normal" looking woman, she does not carry a crystal ball as I half-expected but arrives at my door with a simple gift of a pink rose in hand. Ben takes the kids out while we sit together in my living room and talk as if she were an ordinary person.

Gwen takes out a piece of paper with a line drawing of a woman on it and fills it in with colored pencils. She is drawing me, the colors are my chakras or aura or something. When she finishes, she explains what they mean: the missing piece of my belly relates to the feminine, to my mother. The stuck sadness in my throat to my father. She tells me that he did the best that he could. These words ring true. How had I not seen it before?

Though I can only remember being told that I'm strong and tough, Gwen claims that I'm more sensitive than most, that I've just been hiding it from myself and others. *Is this true? Before the cesarean, I hadn't felt emotional—not since I was a teenager. I thought I had grown beyond this silliness.*

But it is in this session, the first one where I listen instead of talk, where nobody lays hands on me or gives me something to ingest, that things shift. It does not fix the sadness or the pains in my scar, but I do feel as if I can breathe deeply for the first time since the cesarean, maybe for the first time ever.

Almost two years since the cesarean, just as the first crocuses arrive after a long and cold winter, I begin daydreaming of having another baby.

I have gone to every type of practitioner in Ashland. I have been poked, prodded, magneted, and sat upon. I have drunk icky things and denied myself all manner of delicious ones. I have exercised and planned and pushed myself. Has it worked? I have no idea. I have grown to accept the pains in my incision site. Though I still have the vague feeling that something more than the pains is wrong, there seems nothing left to try. I am ready to take on the battle of birth on my terms.

My body must agree, because I immediately miss my period. When the pregnancy test comes up positive, I'm so excited that I send Ben to the store for another package of tests, just to be sure. Though he would have been satisfied trusting the initial results, he remembers how well his refusal to go to the store when I was pregnant with Avram worked out for him. So he grabs the car keys without protest, returning with multiple tests to assure that he won't be sent out again. When the second test comes up positive, I believe it, stashing the others away in the back of the linen closet behind the towels.

We tell Avram there is a baby in my belly. He does not seem impressed or find it worth mentioning to others. This is good because, remembering the multitude of calls and the stress I felt as Avram's due date passed, we decide to wait to tell others about this pregnancy. And this time, I lie about the due date, telling people it is two weeks later than it really is. And, without being asked, I add that I will be having a VBAC.

"Is it safe?" they ask.

Overflowing with statistics, I passionately tell them: "One half of all women who undergo a cesarean suffer complications, and their mortality rate is two to four times higher than those who birth vaginally."[1]

Their eyes dart about looking for an escape.

Quoting Stella, whose midwifery training has made her into a passionate birth activist, I try to make them understand: "Surrounding a woman with masked strangers, putting her on her back with her legs up in the air and shining spotlights on her, and then expecting her to do something as intimate and vulnerable as giving birth is about as logical as expecting a man to ejaculate under the same circumstances."

Like sheep, they cling to comfort: "As long as the doctor says it's okay."

This response infuriates me. *Why is my opinion irrelevant? Doctors may be experts on birth, but I'm the expert of my body. I'm the one who will go through birth. I'm the one whose life and whose baby's life are on the line.*

"Our system is broken," I respond, trying to pull the medical gauze from their eyes. "Medical errors are the sixth leading cause of death in America. Though we spend more than any other country in the world on maternal healthcare,[2] our odds of dying in childbirth are greater here than in forty-nine other countries.[3] And they are getting worse. They have doubled in the last twenty years."[4]

By this point the listener has remembered something that needs his or her immediate attention and makes an excuse to flee.

Don't they understand what is happening? Women are being sacrificed for profits.

I sound, even to myself, like an extremist, like someone who should be featured on *Coast to Coast* or seen standing on a soapbox. It would be so much easier if I could stop thinking and questioning, if I could simply accept and believe, if I could learn to "baaaa."

"Morning sickness" is a horrible misnomer. The nausea in no way confines itself to the morning hours but tortures me throughout the day. I am unable to keep down food, much less prenatal vitamins. I lose weight, though I know I should be eating for two. I am unable to work at Pangea, as the thought of talking about, serving, or smelling food makes my stomach revolt. When Ben returns home after a long day at the restaurant, the smell seeps from his every pore. He must go straight to the shower. His clothes, skipping the hamper, are washed immediately.

My new job, though I don't make any money at it, is lying in bed and focusing on not moving. With Avram's pregnancy there was no real morning sickness, just hours of blissful, uninterrupted sleep. Now that I have a toddler, there is no such thing as uninterrupted sleep. For the first time since he was born, I want nothing to do with Avram. Sometimes he is great about this, allowing me to ignore him while he spends hours carefully lining up his two hundred match-box cars end-to-end in perfect rows. Other times, he tears apart the house, pulling all the tissues out of boxes, playing in the toilet water, and emptying bookshelves. This is okay with me as long as I can stay in bed.

Unless there is a deafening crash, he is on his own. And when there is a crash, unless it is accompanied by loud wailing, I just yell (from the bed): "Stop it." I am especially grateful to Sky Kitty, who seems to find it quite within his role to be pulled around on the wood floor by his tail.

Days pass like this, the house getting dirtier and dirtier, the laundry left undone. It's my mother who finally takes a stand.

"You need to get help. This isn't good for you or the baby," she says.

My stomach attempts to drown her voice in a pool of puke, so she pulls the VBAC card.

"You won't be able to have a VBAC if you aren't strong."

She refers me to Max, a "mad scientist." He lives outside of Talent, a neighboring town so small, it makes Ashland look like a full-sized city. I drag myself out to the car, through Ashland and Talent then down a long dirt driveway to an automatic gate that no longer works. Parking outside the gate, I hike down the drive, past donkeys, geese, chickens, dogs, and cats, to a waiting room where caged hamsters are running circles on wheels. Max is tall with longish wavy brown hair and an easy-going smile. He is wearing a polo shirt, khaki shorts, and Birkenstocks. He offers me a reclining chair in front of a big window, from where, in an attempt to keep my mind off the rolling in my stomach, I watch his children try to corral the chickens.

He puts large, flat circle magnets on my hands and ankles and belly. They are attached, through some sort of rubber-wrapped wire, to another magnet that he puts down his pants. Yes, down his pants. No, not way down to his crotch, but truly, down the front of his pants, below his belly button and (presumably) above his penis.

At this point, I consider leaving. But that would involve getting up, walking across the room and out the door, and I would much prefer to lie here in this comfortable reclining chair and concentrate on not puking.

With the magnet secure in his pants, he makes a pinching motion with his fingers as his hands slowly scan over a tray of small, clear vials. Pinch, pinch, wave, wave. . . . Stopping occasionally, he removes one vial at a time from his tray, eventually narrowing his selection to five or six vials. Holding them out in front of me he explains, "This selection represents things you must completely eliminate from your diet." They include: flour, strawberries, canola oil, nightshades, and soy.

"No problem, I don't want to eat anyway."

"In addition, you must eat more meat and eggs. "

"I'm a vegetarian," I say, assuming he will suggest beans instead.

"Not anymore," he shrugs.

"But I don't believe in eating animals."

"You are suffering from malnourishment. You don't have the protein, energy, or nutrients to nurture you and your baby."

"No, you don't understand. Meat is repulsive to me. I'm not one of those vegetarians who eats veggie burgers and dreams of indulging in the real thing. I am the kind who has absolutely no desire to eat dead things. Ever."

"Eat it anyway," he says, handing me a bill for two hundred dollars.

Though I'm tempted to forget Max and his magnet down his pants and his hand-waving thing, I have a horrible feeling he might be right. Many cultures consider meat strengthening. Though I'm not sure which will be worse, getting it down my throat or experiencing it come back up, I resolve to try.

As disgusted as I am with the idea of eating meat, Ben is delighted at the prospect. Seemingly oblivious to the look of pure misery on my face, he waxes on about all of the dead things he will cook for me.

"Eggs only for now," I insist, reasoning that because I eat bread, cookies, and cakes made with eggs (or used to, until Max told me I couldn't have flour products), it should be no big deal to eat them when they look like eggs.

It being 3:00 in the afternoon doesn't discourage Ben. He scrambles eggs. Straddling a wooden dining room chair turned backwards, he sits across the table from me and watches intently as I push the eggs around on my plate.

These eggs don't look like the ones I have encountered in baked goods. There is no cake texture or frosting. They look like eggs. They smell like eggs. Minimizing the look of revulsion on my face, I take a half-teaspoon-sized bite, chew twice, and quickly swallow. Involuntarily, it comes right back up. I can't help it. It's the smell, something about the disgusting sulfurous stench.

In tears, I drive back to Max's. This time I refuse to hike down the drive but instead force the stupid electric gate open. I'm tempted to leave it that way, but, unsure of what winged and furry creatures might be running around, I close it behind me with more force than necessary.

Max, who is actually a nice chap, hooks me up to the magnets, puts the big one down his pants, does his little wave and pinch routine, gives me a couple of drops of a tasteless liquid, and then disappears into another room. I sit quietly, wondering what the banging and clattering from the other room is, and watch his children swing like monkeys in a large tree smartly fitted with a net, presumably to prevent them from hitting the ground should they fall.

He returns with a bowl of cooked eggs. "Smell them," he says. Tentatively, I take a little sniff. Nothing. Burying my face in the bowl, I inhale deeply and smell. . . . Nothing. They don't smell. I don't know what was in Max's magic drops, and I don't care. They worked, and I'm grateful to this mad scientist and the big magnet in his pants. From that day on, without gagging, I eat eggs every morning for breakfast. I even learn to enjoy them in different forms: deviled, scrambled with feta and tomatoes, and in quiche.

Ben expertly sneaks meat into my food, chopping it into miniscule pieces too small to pick out of soups and adding chicken stock to dishes. It must be good for me because my morning sickness subsides and I am left with more energy than I have had since I was a kid. Returning to Pangea, I resume working regular shifts where, even after hours of staying on my feet, doing dishes, and running plates of food around, I feel strong and energetic.

Without hesitation, Ben and I once again ask Laureen to be our midwife and are delighted when she agrees. A trial of labor is still standard protocol for a woman who has had a cesarean. The only difference is that a second, fully certified midwife will assist Laureen instead of the usual apprentice. Her name is Laura Roe. As the second midwife, we don't see much of her, but she's gregarious and easy to like. We hit it off with her immediately and have no concerns about having her at the birth.

This pregnancy takes on a completely different flavor than the last one. I do not invite anyone to the birth. It will be only the midwives and me and Ben. While appointments for my first pregnancy were full of small talk and chatter, these are serious business. In addition to prenatals, I take vitamins E and C, as they help to strengthen the amniotic sac. I don't want to end up needing to induce because of prolonged membrane rupture again.

We go over Laureen's records and the hospital transcripts from the cesarean line by line. We look for reasons and write lists of "this time." I am dismayed to learn that I was given a single-layer suture. Originally used on sheep, it's a newer and questionable practice used to save time in the operating room. Theoretically, it could increase my chance of uterine rupture, which, though rare (less than 1%),[5] can result in death. I would need immediate surgery. The transport time to the hospital would be too long to assure safety for myself or my baby. I think of my scar and the sharp pains that I still get deep in my core. *Are they a sign that something is wrong?*

For a moment, I contemplate birthing in a hospital. If something went wrong, the hospital would be the best place to be. But being in a hospital can also cause things to go wrong. Statistically, birthing at home will lower the risk of interventions. Interventions lead to complications, which tend to lead to more interventions. I remember how, during my labor, the hospital's bright lights, uniforms, strangers, and infantile rules about candles made me feel. I remember how the contractions slowed each time the nurses or doctor came into the room.

Stella sums it up best: "Don't have anyone at your labor who you wouldn't poop in front of." Though I prefer pooping in private, since Avram came along, doing so is a rare luxury. Avram sees and smells me poop almost every day. He should be at my birth. At the last moment, Mom can bring him.

I don't want to go back to the hospital. I want to be in my own space, surrounded by people I know, trust, and care for. Even though I'm afraid of uterine rupture, I believe the safest option is a natural birth and I know that my best chance for a natural birth is at home.

Ben and I handwrite a release of liability for Laureen's and Laura's files. In it we take full responsibility for the birth and its outcome, stating that no one may hold Laureen or Laura responsible in the event of any complications including mother or infant death.

Recalling my first labor and the way my left brain vacated this world, leaving me detached and at the mercy of strangers whose language and customs I didn't understand, I resolve to write two perfect birth plans, one for home and the other to use in case of hospital transport.

The hospital birth plan is detailed. It specifies, among other things, that as few staff as possible will come and go in the room. I will not be offered pain medication or be asked to change out of my own clothing. No tests, interventions, or procedures will occur without my permission and a midwife consult. The lights are to be kept dim, the hep-lock, used to administer drugs quickly in an emergency situation, delayed until absolutely necessary. I will be examined at minimal intervals and in whatever position I happen to be at the time. My baby's heart tones are to be read only with a Doppler, not an electronic fetal monitor. They will not shave me, strip my membranes, perform an episiotomy, or use forceps, a vacuum, or Cytotec.

In the event a cesarean is advised, a second opinion will be provided and I will be allowed to continue laboring for as long as possible. Unless it's an emergency, I'm to remain awake and alert. Only necessary medical people are to be in the room, no students. My hands are not to be strapped down. My baby's placenta and umbilical cord will remain intact until I decide they are ready to be cut. The baby will be given directly to me to hold, without being cleaned first. The cut will be low and horizontal. It will be closed with double-layer suturing.

These are just the hightlights. My birth plan goes on for five pages, specifying what to do in case of a premature or sick baby, stillbirth, and maternal death. For me, the plan is a relief, a way to reach into the future to take care of myself and my baby, a map to guide my caretakers in case I'm overcome with labor or die. Most of it I copied from birth books, but one rule I came up with on my own: no one but me or Ben is to announce the sex of the baby. After nine months of wondering "boy or girl?" I want to discover this new person on my own.

Though I don't know it, my plan is every obstetrician's worst nightmare. Later, in Dr. Marsden Wagner's wonderful book, *Born in the USA: How a Broken Maternity System Must Be Fixed to Put Women and Children First*,[6] I would come across the Reciprocal Natural Childbirth Index and laugh at my naïveté. (See Table 1 on p. 71) Apparently birth plans, along with hyphenated last names, advanced education, new age music, checking ones own cervix, and driving late model Volvo station wagons, are hilarious and reason enough for doctors to joke about skipping a trial of labor to bind and cut women "during regular working hours."

My home plan is one brief page because most of the details from the hospital plan are irrelevant to a home birth; midwives intervene only as a last resort. The single unusual piece in my home birth plan is: in order to remove the focus on time and progress that hounded me during Avram's birth, Ben will cover all the clocks in the house. The midwives will have watches and pay attention to time and progress. But they will only do minimal checks. With no pressure from external timelines, I trust that my body will follow its own rhythm.

Table 1. THE RECIPROCAL NATURAL CHILDBIRTH INDEX	
Add points as indicated if the woman:	
Goes into labor Friday afternoon	5
Checked (or husband checked) cervix at home	5
Arrives in a late-model Volvo station wagon	5
Has a hyphenated last name	5
Husband has one too	10
Is insured by a managed health care plan	5
Has more than 4 years of college	5
Either parent is a physician	each, add 5
Either parent is an attorney	each, add 10
Insists on calling all staff members by first names	5
Brings own naturopath to assist	5
Has a written birth plan, per page add	5
Spend more than half of labor in the shower	5

Discussion: We have found that a Reciprocal Natural Childbirth index score of 30 or greater should earn the woman in labor immediate consideration for cesarean section. In fact, since you can get a score of 30 without even being in labor, someone with a high enough score could be offered a C-section at her convenience during regular working hours.

Source: A. Berg. "The Reciprocal Natural Childbirth Index," Journal of irreproducible results 36, no. 2 (March/April 1991): 27

Laureen, believing her job is not just to provide a safe birth but also to help grow a family, includes Avram, now a rough-and-tumbly two-year-old with the same thick head of dark hair he was born with, in each prenatal visit. She asks him questions and answers his inquiries about trucks and dogs just as intently as she does mine about babies and birth.

Though the idea of a baby doesn't interest Avram, he thinks the fetoscopes are cool. Laureen brings an extra one just for him. He listens to the baby's heartbeat in my belly, to his own heartbeat in his chest, to the gurgling in his tummy, and, of course, to Sky's tummy as well. Sky Kitty also partakes in the appointments, palpating my belly along with the midwife just as he did when I was pregnant with Avram.

Laureen tells us about a Hypnobirthing class that a local midwife, Rhione, teaches. Hypnobirthing sounds a little like meditation to me. Being an active person, for me sitting still for more than a few moments is not fun. But I've visited a medical intuitive, been hooked up to a magnet down a man's pants, and eaten meat; I can handle Hypnobirthing.

Classes are held in a yoga studio. Rhione, a small woman with a big smile and long, straight, brown-gray hair, sits at the front of a room next to a statue of the Buddha, some candles, and a small vase of flowers. Expectant couples, each having introduced themselves as first-time parents, lie splayed out on giant pillows, listening attentively. A blissful look on her face, Rhione speaks in an airy and musical cadence.

"Labor and birth do not have to hurt." Her eyes seek out contact with every person before continuing Yoda-esquely. "Fear creates tension, which begets pain. By removing fear, we are able to break the cycle. *There is no pain.*"

She invites us to change the language surrounding birth. Instead of "pushing" we are to "breathe our babies down." "Pain" becomes "pressure." "Contractions" are "surges" because the goal is not to contract our bodies but rather to open them and ride the waves. I think the word "wave" is a great description of the experience of labor; like being in the ocean, one's body responds to and navigates an uncontrollable rhythm.

We are told that by simply shifting our focus we can experience pleasurable births. We will practice in class by paying attention to our bodies and our partners during guided meditation. *Yeah right*, I think, looking at the room full of first-time moms. *If you think meditation can mimic birth, you haven't got a chance.* But the others look so hopeful and innocent; I keep my thoughts to myself.

The women arrange big fluffy pillows on their partners' laps, turning them into squishy sorts of chairs. Ben holds me while reading Rhione's script in a steady monotone. "There is a clock. Watch the second hand turn. With each movement it brings you deeper. You breathe into your toes, feeling them become light and almost float. Good. Now breathe into your legs. . . ."

My first inclination is to laugh. My second to get up and do something. I'm too hyperactive to truly want to do this. But, following Ben's voice, I try to relax into the pillows. "Envision your baby gently moving into your yoni [Sanskrit for vagina, especially as a divine passage or sacred temple]. Imagine your yoni opening like a rose bud. See the petals of the rose slowly and easily unfolding and opening, allowing the baby to slip out."

She goes on describing birth in ways I've never imagined. My mind quiets, though, unlike the others, I don't "leave the room." But I do begin to see that my body's response does not have to be instinctual. I can choose my own reaction. Instead of tensing against "pressure," I can observe it and simply allow myself to be uncomfortable. I can choose to pay attention to Ben holding me and the good feelings that brings up instead of focusing on the pressure. And if I follow his voice as he reads the script, I can let go of some of what's happening in the room and to my body. It doesn't leave completely; it just fades the same way thoughts of unappealing men do when a gorgeous hunk walks through the door.

At the end of class, Rhione shows us a video of a Hypnobirth. We laugh at the astonished look on the doctor's face as his head bobs from the fetal monitor, which shows intense contractions, to the laboring woman who seems completely unaffected by the contractions, almost as if she is asleep. Though her composure amazes me, I don't want this kind of birth. It reminds me of being drugged during Avram's delivery. I want to be active and up and about in labor. Even though having a Hypnobirth is not my goal, I think the language Rhione offers is great.

To be sure that the placenta isn't located over my uterine scar, which could lead to dangerous complications, I agree to Laureen's recommendation and arrange to have a partial ultrasound. At the beginning of the appointment I hand the technician Laureen's orders for "placenta location only." Seeing that the technician is probing not just around the scar but all over my belly, I ask, "What are you doing?"

"Just checking fetal size," she replies nonchalantly.

"No. I only want to know if the placenta is on top of my scar."

"There's a whole routine we do. We need to make sure the fetal growth is on schedule and the heart is pumping properly."

My midwife can do that with her hands and fetoscope, I think. "My provider wrote 'placenta location only' on the order," I tell her.

"It's policy."

"It's *my* body."

Meeting my eyes with hers for the first time, she says, "I'll have to ask." Exhaling loudly, she stands and leaves the room. She and her co-workers mill around for a while discussing the "crazy, hormonal, pregnant lady who won't let them do their job." (Okay, I wasn't actually close enough to hear them, but the impression is so vivid in my mind that I'm sticking to my story.) Meanwhile, I lie there fuming that the medical system assumes the authority to make decisions about my body.

The tech, returning with a form attached to a clipboard, says, "You'll have to sign this AMA form." The form specifies that I'm leaving against medical advice and that horrible things like death or disability for me or my fetus may result. Ironically, these are the same possible side affects I had to approve when I agreed to the cesarean. Either way, whether I do what I want or what they want me to, they won't be held responsible.

While my pregnancy with Avram seemed to drag on forever, now that I have a toddler to keep me occupied, the nine months pass quickly. As the due date nears, Mom, Stella, and my friends from the weekly moms' group offer to make a blessing way for me. I refuse. Ben and Laureen are the only ones that I speak freely with. I don't want encouragement or kindness from friends who have birthed vaginally. Though kind, supportive and genuine, they can't understand. Well, maybe they could, but I don't want them to. I don't want anyone to know that the cesarean broke me. Mom makes mochi by herself and arranges it prettily on a plate with a short vase of fresh flowers for me.

Ben gets a belly cast kit. He and Avram rub Vaseline all over my belly and breasts. Avram delights in this, as it clearly qualifies as playing with one's food. They then layer strips of paper-mache over me. In short but itchy time, the entire mass hardens to an accurate replica of a very pregnant me, complete with a right breast that is double the size of the more recently nursed left breast. Representing eighty-five pounds more than I usually weigh, this model of my round belly and enormous breasts remains one of my most favorite treasures.

8 A Window

On January 20th, at 4:30 am—two weeks after my due date, just like with Avram's birth—I awake to my water breaking. *I guess taking vitamins C and E was a waste,* I think, remembering the bottles of pills I had taken to try to prevent early rupture of membranes. Though this is a little discouraging, the regular yet mild surges that begin soon after give me hope. They become especially strong when I nurse Avram.

At 7:00 pm, Laureen comes to check on me. The surges are four minutes apart. The baby's heart tones are great, and my vitals are all normal. She does not do an internal exam. Instead, under the guise of reading *The Little Mouse, the Red Ripe Strawberry, and the Big Hungry Bear* to Avram, she watches. The surges feel easy and manageable to me, but Laureen decides to stay. This is how I know that I'm truly in labor. It's really happening.

I continue working with the surges. Mom takes Avram to her house for the night. I walk around my home and yard, stopping with each surge for Ben to support my two-hundred-plus pounds of weight while I will my body to relax, to open. Ben is fabulous. Not once does he say "I've got you." Our Hypnobirthing routine works well. I don't experience "pain," the surges continue to be manageable.

At 11:00 pm, the second midwife, Laura, arrives. The two give me space, coming close only occasionally to coax me to drink or give Ben a short break. I am calm and relaxed, enjoying the labor.

As the surges intensify, Laureen and Laura light candles around the hot tub I am using as a birthing tub this time. Floating in the water, surrounded by my support team, I'm able to soften, open, and breathe through the surges. It is not until the still-dark early morning hours that Laureen makes her first check on the baby's position to find that my cervix is almost fully dilated. "Your baby's head is right here," she says. Putting a hand between my legs, I reach inside myself and, stretching as far as I can, I feel my baby's soft hair. Inches to birth. Inches to my arms.

But when mid morning arrives and I still have no urge to "breathe my baby out," my patience dwindles. I'm tired of laboring, of Hypno-birthing, of Ben, Laureen, Laura, and of being in labor. I'm exhausted and want to sleep, but the surges won't let me.

Along with each surge, my legs uncontrollably cramp up. While not painful, the cramps are annoying and invasive. There is nothing rhythmic about them. They command my attention, rendering me unable to relax. In the moments when it is most important for me to be with the surges, the leg cramps take me out. I am unable to "breathe through the surges" no matter what Ben in his suddenly infuriating Hypnobirthing voice, reciting the stupid Hypnobirthing script, says. Though my vitals and the baby's vitals remain good, my attitude is not.

The midwives, taking pity on Ben, relieve him. Suspecting that the baby is in a posterior, or "sunny side up" position, they try to manually move the baby back into place by holding my body, hammock style in a sheet, with my feet higher than my head, while Laureen, her entire hand up inside of my vagina, tries to turn the baby over. This does not work. It does hurt. A lot.

At 11:00 am, at my request, Laureen calls an acupuncturist to help get things going. The acupuncturist refuses to come, saying I have been in labor too long. So we call Max, the mad scientist with the big magnet. He comes right over and physically adjusts my thigh, relieving the cramping, which, in turn, reduces my whining, much to Ben's and the midwives' relief.

To increase the surges, Max feeds me a thick, sweet herbal tincture with Chinese lettering on it. (Days later I will find the original box with its English identification: "100% pure frog extract.") Though the frog juice increases my energy, I still have no urge to "breathe my baby out."

I use every trick the midwives can think of to increase the surges. Leaving the tub, I walk the yard, pace the house, and go up and down stairs.

"Verbalize," Laureen tells me. "Embody a lion."

I roar with all my might.

Avram misses me. Mom, who has been caring for him, is unable to reach us by phone, so she brings him over unannounced. He is wide-eyed and scared to see his pacing, groaning mother. He wants me, but I don't know how to handle the surges and be present to him at the same time. Though I will later regret not being strong enough to reassure him and once again failing him in birth, I send my son away. But the memory of his wide eyes and tears doesn't leave me; it's there always.

At 6:00 pm on January 21st, a day and a half since my membranes ruptured, labor began, and I last slept, Laureen and Laura recommend hospital transport. I refuse. So they offer to try some guided pushing.

I lie on a folded futon. Laureen, seated across from me, says, "Take a deep breath and push."

This is the one and only moment when my labor resembles what TV tries to pass off as labor. Except of course that I am naked, in my own home, and two uniform-free women are attending me.

"Good. Take a breath and try again. "

I try. I do. But it does no good. My baby isn't budging.

By 9:45 pm, my contractions, though painful (sorry, Hypnobirthing people, it's been a day and a half; surely they qualify as contractions and as painful by now) are clearly not accomplishing anything. The midwives reiterate that they believe I need to transport. I am free to do what I want, but they will not stay at home with me anymore.

Briefly, I consider staying home alone. But I don't know what to do differently and have no idea what I would do if I were successful in delivering a baby. Seeing no other option, I agree to transport.

Comforting myself with the knowledge that babies are born vaginally in hospitals all the time, I decide to ask the doctor for some drugs, just enough to cut the pain, just enough to grant me an hour or two of sleep. Then I will have the strength to push again.

We transport to a different hospital this time. The midwives are relieved to hear that the doctor on call is Diane Vikson. They have worked with her before and hold her in high regard. This soothes me.

Ben drives me to the hospital and drops me off in front of the ER. Breathing into the surges, I gather my mental capacities before waddling into the big building alone, my hospital birth plan gripped tightly in hand. Everything is glaring and bright.

Handing the nurse my insurance card (one uninsured baby was enough for me, thank you), I say, "I have been in active labor for a day and a half. I am dilated to nine centimeters. The baby is in plus-2 position. There has been no progress for twelve hours. My contractions are no longer effective."

I'm a bit smug at the nurse's response. Eyes bulging, mouth hanging open just like the doctor in the Hypnobirthing movie, she is in shock that I'm up and walking when I should be lying on a table moaning and groaning. "Get a wheelchair!" she hollers.

"No," I silence her. *I will not be pushed around.* "I want to walk." *I will keep power over my body. I will stay in control in this shiny place of strangers.*

They do not have a clean room ready. So I sit, my baby's head a bowling ball between my legs. Not wanting to interact with others, I look at the floor and will my body to relax and open. I refuse to think of the last time I was in a hospital.

Instead, I watch feet walk by. The nurses, their white sneakers peeking out from green pants, hurry by without pause, while maintenance people seem to walk purposefully slowly. Patients and visitors amble, pausing, turning, sometimes backtracking. Phones ring. A baby cries. The nurse coming on duty is teased about her new boyfriend. Another complains about the hospital's computer system. I do not voice my desperation for a room but sit and, every four minutes, exhale slowly, squeezing Ben's hand.

Finally, I am given my own room. Soft lights. Relief. I lie down on my side. A nurse, without asking my permission or checking my birth plan, hooks me up to a monitor and sets up a hep-lock in my hand.

Dr. Vikson enters the room. She is petite with shoulder-length light brown hair. There is nothing imposing, frenetic or doctorish about her. Her voice and movements are minimal and contained. Though the nurses, Ben, Laureen, and the machines are still present, somehow they slip into the background. The room feels vast, like high-mountain Colorado air on a windless day. This effect comes from her. This seemingly fragile doctor-woman seems to make space instead of taking it up.

"I love your restaurant," she says, taking the time to get to know me. "My children's babysitter, Therese, used to work for you."

"Please," I interrupt. Though I appreciate her intent to make small talk before she sticks her hand inside my vagina, my mind can focus on only one subject at a time. Now, it's the one jammed into my pubic bone.

She quiets, allowing me to interrupt her, waiting for me to find words. I have her complete attention. She is not formulating her next sentence or thinking of anything else; she is simply waiting.

"Please, give me something to help me sleep. If I can rest for an hour, I will be able to keep going."

"Just a moment," she replies and closes her eyes. This is not the response I expect. I don't know what she is doing, but I am grateful that she is not rushing about, ordering tests, or using big doctor words. As we sit in silence, my fear of her lessens.

Opening her eyes, she gently says, "I don't believe it's safe to continue. It's been too long and the baby is in some distress. . . ."

"No." Again, she allows me to interrupt her. "I don't need to sleep, I'll take Pitocin. I'm fine. Really. Give me Pitocin, or Cytotec even. I can do this."

She waits for many moments of silence to follow my words. She waits until we both know that I've finished speaking. "It's not safe. You need a cesarean." Though still gently spoken, there is an authority in her voice I had not heard until now.

No! I panic. Though my lips stay pressed together, *Do not cut me!* screams through my body. I'm certain she's heard my thoughts.

She answers, not unkindly, with her eyes: *There is no room for negotiation.*

"I want another opinion."

"I will call someone for you," she agrees. Her voice is tender, loving almost. It's horrible. I don't want her to be nice. I want someone to fight. Someone to blame. Someone to hate.

I dismiss her by looking away. The nurses follow her. The room and the machines once again close in on me. The contractions are slow, painful, but petering out. They too are giving up on me.

Another doctor comes in. She is young. She rambles on, talking circularly in general terms of theories, possibilities, and consequences. She talks and she talks and she talks but never seems to get to a point.

I don't want to have to think about or understand anything. I just want to know what I can do besides submit. After two midwives have passed me off to a doctor who insists on a cesarean, I figure all I need is a different doctor to keep doing whatever it is they do with their little Dopplers and Pitocin or fetal monitors or forceps or whatever, anything but a cesarean, anything. Frustrated with this one's blabber, I ask, "What can you do?"

"I can't do anything," she replies, "I don't have privileges."

Devastated, I ask, "Who does?"

"Dr. Vikson is the only one here."

It is over. I'm at the most mother-friendly hospital in the area, under the care of the most alternative doctor they have. No other options exist. I concede, signing my name to the liability waiver, the one saying that I understand the risks of cesarean include infection, hemorrhage, low Apgar, cutting of the baby, breathing problems, injury to organs, adhesions, and maternal and/or infant death.

Knowing how badly I wanted to avoid this, Ben asks that we be left alone for a while. He cries for me. Holding my hand, he speaks words of love and pride at all my hard work. He tries to connect to me, but I'm not there anymore. He is speaking to an empty shell.

At 2:30 am, the uniforms come back. With their gowns and masks and gloves on, it's not possible to tell one from the other—not that it matters. As they wheel me into the operating room, I think again of dying. It does not scare me but settles upon me with a strangely comfortable familiarity. I've done this before. It would be simple to slip away. To just stop. Stop the pain. Stop the failure. Stop the shame.

The drugs they use this time are different. They do not churn in my stomach. The doctors allow both Ben and Laureen to stay with me. I am thankful for this, even while noting, cynically, how quickly I have fallen from being queen of my own castle-home, with freedom to do whatever I wanted, to this: a serf, grateful that I'm not throwing up, that I'm "allowed" to have two people accompany me while I'm cut open.

In all fairness, these uniforms are great (for uniforms). They are compassionate in their speech and touch. If one must be bound, cut open, and have one's innards taken out, it's helpful when the uniforms doing the cutting are kind.

My nostrils fill with the smell of burning flesh—my flesh burning. It's all too familiar. As in a recurring nightmare, I know what will follow. There is a violent pulling apart deep where no separation should be. *You can breathe*, I tell myself as the same unbearable pressure descends on my lungs. I hear plastic rustling, a sucking noise, and the steady beep of a monitor in the background. Ben's blue eyes steadily embrace mine.

Dr. Vikson, removing my baby, hands the baby off to a uniform who announces "I have him." With these three words, a stranger in a white coat, oblivious to my meticulously prepared birth plan, the one specifying that the baby's gender not be spoken, has announced the arrival of our son, Jonah.

Quickly they suction him and, conceding to my most important request, lay him on my bare chest to warm. Ben arranges the blankets to block the bright lights, a cave for just the two of us. While Dr. Vikson continues to work on my open belly, I meet my baby. We are given a few minutes of the most precious sweetness I have ever experienced. Looking into his eyes, I forget what is happening to my body.

My Jonah is beautiful. Calm and peaceful with a downy coat of light hair, he looks at me. I am grateful for the gift of this profound time, to be the first person my baby sees, to allow the familiar beat of my heart to comfort him, and to have the dignity, privacy and warmth of my little cave—a small sanctuary from the outside world where the rest of my body, fully exposed, is being manually stripped of its placenta, suctioned, and stitched.

When the pediatrician arrives, he is angry. "Prolonged membrane rupture and a meconium-exposed baby? Why didn't you call me immediately?!" he demands. It's only now, writing this, that I realize Dr. Vikson went out on a limb to gift me with these dear bonding moments.

Without meeting my eyes, telling me where he is going, or what he will do, he takes Jonah and leaves the room.

"Go," I say to Ben. Though I will miss his blue eyes, it is more important that our baby is not alone with a stranger.

Laureen stays with me. I close my eyes and pray for the procedure to be over soon. It's not. It lasts much longer than my first cesarean.

Released to the recovery room, I wait for Ben to return with Jonah. I'm grateful that, this time, the drugs do not drag me into unwanted sleep and when my baby arrives, that my arms are strong enough to hold him. I am amazed at how, even at an hour young, he is totally different than Avram. Jonah is skinny with a thin layer of light brown hair on his head, while Avram was chunky with thick dark hair. Though Jonah is just one ounce lighter than Avram was, he seems so little, so fragile. I do not remember Avram being this small. But it's not only his appearance that's different; his soul is. I hadn't known that the essence of who we are is written before birth.

I offer my breast to him, but he wants to look into my eyes instead. He watches me closely and mimics my facial expressions, as newborns are known to do in these sacred and alert hours just after birth. I look back into his eyes and I tell him that I love him and am glad he is here.

Mom and Avram arrive to meet baby Jonah. I see fear and confusion in Avram's eyes. He does not run to me as he usually would. Physical pains constrict my heart to witness such a change in him. He looks years older. Having been the center of our world, rarely leaving our sides, he has just spent two days without us, broken only by a brief glimpse of me in pain. I had not prepared him for the hospital, for the monitors and tubes coming out of my body. And there on his throne (my lap) is a small stranger.

Instead of proudly showing Jonah off to Mom, I pass him over to her quickly, trying to appear nonchalant to Avram's absorbing stare. Keeping my eyes on Avram, I ask, "Will you come sit with me?"

Releasing my mother's hand, he walks across the room.

Ben lifts him onto the bed, explaining: "Mama can't lift you now. She has an owie on her belly. We have to be careful to not touch it or even to wiggle."

Out of the corner of my eye, I see my mother crying in joy while meeting her beautiful, healthy grandbaby, but I keep my attention on Avram. "I missed you so much, and I'm so happy to see you. Do you know how much I love you?" I ask, ruffling his hair.

Wide-eyed, he nods.

"All these tubes and things will be gone soon, and then I can come home with you." I wrap my arms around and press him to me, holding my breath so as to not cry out from the pain it causes. Closing my eyes, I continue silently, thinking the words this two-year-old isn't yet ready to hear:

I'm so sorry. I wanted this to be different for you. I wanted you to experience a good birth, to watch your brother come into our family peacefully. But once again I was not strong enough to hold you close through birth. Once again you missed me and cried for me, and once again I was not there for you. I'm sorry my son.

I do not indulge in tears. Instead, I fill my body with rage at itself for not birthing this baby, for failing again.

Mom brings Jonah over to meet Avram. Sitting cross-legged, Avram holds him ever so briefly for a photo. He does not smile.

I nurse them together, one on each breast. A serious look on his face, Avram resists as long as possible, but Jonah's sweetness is too much for even Avram to deny. Eventually he reaches across me to hold Jonah's hand. We fall asleep this way, the three of us squished together in the narrow hospital bed. Ben carries Avram four feet away to a hard window seat, where they spend what's left of the night.

Hours later, I wake to find this beautiful angel still in the crook of my arm. Touching his toes, which grab my finger back with dexterity, I kiss and nuzzle him awake. He smiles at me. Experts claim that newborns don't smile; they pass gas which contorts their face. But I don't buy that. He loves me and is happy to see me. Ben, waking from the cramped window seat, leaves with Avram to make breakfast, shower, and take care of the details of life that do not wait for labor.

Dr. Vikson comes to check on me. "How are you?"

"That depends. What does a woman need to do to give birth the right way?" I'm trying to make light of my insolence last night.

Though she can see that I'm not capable of getting out of bed, much less conceiving in the near future, she does not laugh or brush away the question. Sitting in a chair next to me, she closes her eyes and pauses for many moments, as if listening to someone or something else. Opening them, she gently says, "I don't think it would be safe for you to have a vaginal birth. The bridge of your pelvis is very short."

"Lots of women who have been told that have gone on to have successful VBACs."

Tilting her head slightly to the right and gentling her voice even more, she tells me: "Roanna, during the surgery, inside of you, I found more adhesions than I have ever seen."

This silences me.

"Adhesions are internal scars, strand-like tissues. They stuck your uterus to other organs and parts of your body. I took the time to remove all that I could. I put a special type of a sheet around your uterus to discourage new adhesions. The sheet will eventually break down and disappear."

"Were they here?" I ask, touching the right side of my scar where the sharp pains from Avram's cesarean still haunt me.

"No, here," she says, putting her hand on the upper left part of my belly, far from the incision. Her hand in place, her eyes never wavering from mine, she continues, "You labored for so long that your uterus pulled a two-to-three-centimeter hole in itself. You needed this cesarean."

My eyes fill in silent response. *If she hadn't intervened, I would be dead.* In my mind's eye, I see my uterus, torn and broken: a physical demonstration of my inadequacy as a woman.

Dr. Vikson continues, "The pediatrician is worried that due to prolonged rupture of the membranes coupled with meconium exposure, your baby may possibly have an infection. He wants blood drawn to see if antibiotics are needed."

Ben returns, and wheels me and Jonah into another room, where a nurse is waiting to draw the blood. At her instruction, I lay Jonah on a metal table. Ben and I hold his arms down and his body still as the nurse takes out a long needle and inserts it into his arm, prodding to find a vein. She misses. Jonah, who until now has only been calm and peaceful, screams with all his might: loud, piercing screams with no break between them.

Again she tries and misses. Jonah turns blue. There is no break in his screaming. We hold him still, our hands forcing his little body to succumb while our voices try to penetrate his terror and beg absolution for the cruel actions of our hands.

A third time she goes in, pushing around inside his small arm, looking for a vein. Jonah, his screams having gone unanswered, shuts down, his body completely limp. He is silent, somewhere else. I cry.

The nurse continues to dig around inside his seemingly lifeless arm. Our hands, no longer needing to constrict him, now stroke and love him. Finally finding the vein, she draws a vial of blood almost as large as his forearm.

The test results are good. Jonah is healthy.

Other than this, Jonah does not cry or fuss but spends his first days sleeping, nursing, and occasionally waking to poop or smile at me. Like new lovers, we are content to do nothing but explore each other's eyes.

The hard way, I remember cesarean recovery coping strategies: I use arm strength only to shift positions, consciously softening my abdomen so as not to engage my stomach muscles. Before coughing or sneezing, I cover the incision with a pillow to prevent my insides from coming out. (The nurse's claim they won't, but I'm the one feeling it, and I tell you that is exactly what is happening.) I do not, under any circumstances, laugh.

The nurses spend an inordinate amount of time making sure my bodily functions work properly—a testament to my inability to do anything right. They bring a bag contraption to monitor my breathing, and their favorite question is: "Have you farted yet?"

The hospital room fills with flowers and cards. A balloon arrangement arrives with big smiling faces on the balloons and the word "congratulations" written on one. I know that these gifts from loved ones across the country are sent with only good intentions, yet a small, spiteful voice in my mind is angry that people are celebrating when my body has just been bound and violated. Trying to impose reason, I tell the voice: *Shut up. Go away. Leave me alone.* It persists, its shrill accusations echoing around my mind. The Mylar balloons bounce gently on their strings as their surfaces reflect in each other and in the hospital mirror, multiplying into hundreds of Mylar faces grinning at me.

The next day, the nurses want me to pee. Holding me up, they help to align my body carefully so pounds support pounds. The stomach muscles necessary for balance have disappeared. Taking minuscule sliding steps without lifting my feet, I travel the ten feet to the bathroom, where I successfully pee, then travel ten feet back to rest from the effort.

On the third day, when I squeeze out a small squirt of poop, the nurses are so pleased, you would think I had solved world hunger. With this momentous event, I am allowed to go home, where I fall into bed, exhausted and cuddled close to my beautiful Jonah boy: so small, so perfect. The beneficiary of his older brother's tireless determination to make ours a family bed, Jonah sleeps on a lambskin in the crook of my arm. Tangled together, the four of us sleep through the night, though I half-wake Jonah occasionally to coax him to nurse on my readily available breast.

I had heard that when the second child comes, the first becomes an afterthought. It is not this way for me. Jonah's needs are easily met, while Avram's are big and complex.

Until now, Avram had been the center of everything. Now there is a brother who takes up his parents' time and attention, who sleeps in his mother's arms. Guests who used to fuss over him pass by without a word to "coo" over Jonah. Though Mom and I laugh over Avram's confiding to her "I want to poke holes in him and throw him in the pool," I feel bad that this transition is so difficult for him.

Sacrificing my own useless body, I defy the doctor's and my mother's orders, regularly lifting Avram into my arms. I crave the hurt, using it to cleanse my guilt for not birthing as a woman should. Grateful that Jonah is easy, I give Avram all the attention I can and worry that it is not enough.

I continue to be surprised by the contrast between my two boys. Whereas Avram as a newborn belonged to the world and was content with anyone's attention, Jonah belongs to me and me alone. Other people are interesting, but when he wants me, no one else will do. We are in love.

Jonah's expressions are huge. They require his entire face and lots of concentration to make: his eyebrows, nose, cheeks, chin, lips, and eyes all working together to get his point across. He is a "good" baby. Though I hate that term—How could a baby be bad?—it's true. He rarely cries. I shift between wishing he could stay a baby forever and eagerly anticipating who he will become as he grows up.

Avram doesn't like to hold Jonah, but he enjoys telling me what to do. "Jonah needs blankets," or "Jonah is hungry," he instructs me. I indulge him, recognizing that it is his way of finding his new place as the big kid.

"At least you and the baby are healthy," friends and family say. I lift the corners of my mouth in silent submission, ignoring my heart's protest: *Birth is not an accident, to be celebrated when you make it through alive. Birth is a rite of passage. There was something I was supposed to do. I am not strong enough to bring life into this world, not good enough. I am unworthy of procreation. Incomplete. An actor playing the role of a woman.*

I had convinced myself that my first cesarean was "their" fault. Surely if I had eaten more, slept longer, or had a birth plan, I would have been able to birth naturally. By educating myself and fighting for it during my second pregnancy, I would succeed. But I was wrong. If science hadn't intervened, I would be dead.

Laureen tries to talk to me about the birth. She wants to process and support, to help me understand. I refuse. I'm angry—angry at everyone, but especially, myself. I gave everything I could and it didn't work. What's the use of talking about it? The violation of my body is an acceptable price to pay for a healthy newborn.

Unlike after the first cesarean, this time I do not wake in the middle of the night in tears. I choose numbness. I will not complain or fight or cry. It is over. I am thankful for the healthy children that the doctors gave me. I am a mother, a wife, a boss. I will not allow anything else to matter. Just like Jonah accepted the needle, I will accept the cesarean. It is over.

And so it has been for more than a year. Over. I haven't talked about Jonah's entry into the world. I haven't even thought about birth, until now, these soft April days following that silly Orgasmic Amazon Queen Sex, which seems to have left me all aflutter.

It must be hormonal, this daydreaming of a little girl. Why would I want to host another person in my body for nine months, to increase my body weight by 40 percent while giving up simple pleasures like a glass of wine and the flexibility to easily wipe my own butt? And after all that, I would still have to get the baby out.

Filling the prescription the pediatrician handed me is the logical thing to do.

Instead I prop it up on my dresser. Sometimes I put it inside a drawer. Sometimes I carry it in my pocket. The one thing I never do is fill it.

If I were to acknowledge my fancies, I would confess I'm holding out hope that the completely irrational but beautiful experience was real. And even though I'm not the sort of person who has intuitive, come-to-goddess experiences, taking a pill that would prevent the possibility of being that kind of person—now that would be dumb.

So it's with purposeful indifference that, two and a half weeks after Orgasmic Amazon Queen Sex, I take a pregnancy test. I'm not exactly sure when to expect my period, but I am good at math. Since fertility occurs two weeks before a cycle, either I'm pregnant now or Orgasmic Amazon Sex happened before I was fertile. Luckily, there is an unused pregnancy test hiding behind the towels in the linen closet. It's only slightly expired.

One pink line. I'm not pregnant.

I'm relieved. Really. I am. Though I did love being pregnant: my stomach growing big, the pleasure of letting it all hang out, feeling beautiful and round at the same time, the wonder of a baby wiggling and rolling inside my body, alive, just inches below my skin but worlds away. A little girl would have been sweet.

9 The Lie

Dr. Vikson's office has sent me a routine reminder that I am due for a pap, so I make an appointment. I haven't seen her since twelve days after the cesarean, now more than a year ago, when she wrote in her report "though the patient seriously desires a VBAC, I advise against it."

Though I like Dr. Vikson very much, given our history—my insistence on birthing vaginally, followed by an excessively long surgery during which she had to slice through a nest of adhesions and sew up a hole where my womb started to rip open—I am nervous about the appointment. I imagine she thinks I'm one of those anti-medicine, home birth quacks. Which I am. But this will be a pap, not a delivery. There shouldn't be much to have differing opinions about today.

I haven't had been to an ob-gyn for an annual exam before. Laureen did them for me, but she is no longer practicing midwifery. I feel a little uncomfortable. Filling out the paperwork on autopilot, my mind wanders: *What should I call her? Doctor? Diane? Dr. Vikson?* "Dr. Vikson" seems so formal. This is the person who cut my body open and took out my son. I should be able to call her Diane.

The nurses weigh me, take a urine sample, and ask intimate questions. (How awkward is this: a stranger asking about my last period, and I'm in nothing but a blue paper towel they have the nerve to call a gown.) The nurse wants to know if I have anything to discuss with Dr. Vikson.

I figure this is my business and say "No," deciding then and there to call her Diane.

Dr. Vikson enters the room wearing a pastel blue blouse over a long skirt. Mary Jane–style clogs peek out from underneath the hem. Her shoulder-length hair hangs simply over dangly earrings. She's doesn't look like a doctor. (Relief.) Chickening out, I avoid the title completely and greet her with "Hi."

"How have you been?" she asks. Then she waits. She doesn't look around the room or at her chart. She just looks in my eyes and waits. I can see that she remembers me and truly wants to know. More important, I feel that in spite of the events surrounding Jonah's birth, she doesn't dislike me.

Settling into the chair, I respond the way I always do when someone asks me how I am: with answers about the people and things in my life. "Everything's great. Jonah's a year old now. Pangea is busy."

Smiling at my maneuver, she looks at my chart and then asks, "Is there any chance you are pregnant?"

"No," I reply, my heart silently finishes the sentence: *but last week, I thought I was pregnant with a little girl.*

We are interrupted by a quick rap on the door. It opens to an anonymous hand offering up a piece of paper. Apologizing, Dr. Vikson takes it and, without pause, turns to show me. It's covered in writing, but something on the bottom left stands out. It's a small plus sign, and it's circled.

My voice and mind freeze, mouth agape. My heart, deep inside, grins. *You are going to have a baby girl*, it whispers.

"That's wonderful," I say aloud. Not thinking about the delivery, I mean it.

Dr. Vikson searches my eyes to assure herself that I'm truly happy about this pregnancy before smiling and hugging me back. She seems so excited for me that it's hard to believe she does this sort of thing on a daily basis.

As I check out afterwards, the receptionist asks when (not if) I would like to return for my prenatal exam. *Baaaa*, I make an appointment.

Driving home, I wonder why I did so. *Is making a prenatal appointment with a doctor setting myself up to have a hospital birth? Do I want a hospital birth?* While chances are I will end up with one, does that mean I want to start there? The idea of scheduling a cesarean, of not fighting, seems temptingly easy. *Could it be a "success,"* I wonder, *if I accept it now, instead of fighting for and losing a natural birth?*

I arrive home to chaos. The boys are running around screaming. Ben is attempting to work on the computer. This is not the right time to share. I hold my secret close while making dinner.

Together around the table, we hold hands and sing:

> *Welcome, welcome, welcome to our table.*
> *Welcome, welcome, we all join hands together*
> *Love in our hearts*
> *Peace on earth*
> *And good friends all around the table.*

There is a moment of quiet. Not out of respect but because the boys' little mouths are too full to speak. Ben, while reaching for the bread, asks, "How was your appointment?"

"I'm pregnant."

His hand stops midair, a look of disbelief on his face. Then he is laughing. We are both laughing.

"You are pregnant," he echoes.

Forgetting food, we sit there holding hands, looking into each other's eyes and beaming. *We are going to have a baby. This baby is wanted. This family is precious. Nothing else matters.*

The bliss lasts only a few minutes, until the boys, satiated, grow restless. Food begins flying, and we return to parenting the loud, messy children of the present.

It's not until later, with the boys fast asleep, Jonah snoring softly, that I sit with my hands on my belly and imagine the little baby inside me. "Welcome," I whisper. I think of the smell of a baby's breath and the way the toes curl around and grasp the touch of my fingertips. I think of itty-bitty socks and lambskins and slings.

But no matter how I try to focus on the baby, fear, lapping relentlessly at the corners of my mind, taunts me: *This baby is going to grow and become big and you are going to have to get it out.* Scheduling a cesarean would tame this stupid voice in my head. But how can I allow myself to be tied down and cut open without a fight?

If I can just ignore the fear, I can be brave and strong. Pulling on my armor, I brace myself to pulverize any sign of self-weakness. *I will act in spite of fear. When I feel its frigid shadow grasping at my thoughts, I will push it away.*

But fear, by its very nature, only grows larger when threatened.

Since Laureen is no longer practicing midwifery, I am both sad and excited at the prospect of a fresh start. Without considering other options, I call Laura Roe, the midwife who assisted Laureen during my pregnancy with Jonah.

Laura, being in the business of attending births, knows exactly why I am calling. Regardless, we do the small talk first.

"It's been a while. How long has it been?" she asks.

"A little more than a year."

"How are the kids?

"They are great, and yours?"

"Doing well. Maya just started school."

"That's nice. This spring weather sure is great."

"Yes it certainly is. . . ."

But small talk is so not my thing. I don't really care how long it's been or that Maya is in school. This is about me. So I cut her off, blurting out: "I'm pregnant and I want to have a VBAC. Will you be my midwife?"

"Congratulations," she says. But there is no joy in her voice.

A pause, more pregnant than I am, ensues.

I remember our last conversation. *Why didn't I think of it before?* It was right after Jonah was delivered. She advised me to give my scar two years to heal before getting pregnant again, advice I have obviously ignored. *But I didn't mean to get pregnant.* Opening my mouth to articulate this, I realize that an irresponsible pregnancy won't help my case.

Why doesn't she say anything?

"Will you consider working with me? I ask again. "I live right next to the hospital now, so if we need to transport it will be simple. I have been in to see Dr. Vikson already. I will work with her as well, so I can have hospital support just in case."

Carefully and without enthusiasm she responds: "I'm going out of town for six weeks. Let's discuss it when I get back."

Postponing thoughts of labor and birth for six weeks works for me. I focus instead on the baby growing in my belly. I share the news with family and friends. Avram is not interested. After all, the last baby turned into a toddler who follows him everywhere, plays with his toys, and messes up his meticulous lines of matchbox cars. But Jonah, just a few months past his first birthday, is thrilled. Multiple times a day he lifts my shirt, saying "baby" while he lovingly touches and kisses my belly. *Can he possibly understand that another person in there?* I wonder.

Dad comes for a visit. While he's here, I invite Mom over for dinner and we all share a meal together. There is no fighting. No sarcasm or sharp jabs. Apparently they have moved on. Traces of their battle-filled past seem to exist only inside of me.

The boys had met my father a couple of times before. But now that they are older, they can better appreciate his sense of humor and even join in the fun. The three of them find it hilarious to put vegetable sticks in their noses and ears, to talk in funny high-pitched voices, and to wave at strangers driving past, as if they are long-lost friends. When the dish soap goes missing, I find it and the three of them on the trampoline. They have added water from the garden hose and are jumping—Dad and Avram fully clothed, Jonah buck-naked—in mountains of suds.

My children's' delight in my dad challenges my own view of him. Memories of his love and support, long buried underneath those difficult teenage years, resurface. I realize that my father has always been generous and loving. He just has his own way and timeline. I accept, for the first time, that though his calls are months apart and visits even rarer, my father loves me.

When Dad leaves, we take a trip to the coast with Mom. She loves the ocean the way a child does. She does not sit quietly or gather shells on dry sand. Mom greets the ocean with wild abandon, running into its frigid waters, arms outstretched, sing-shouting "hellooooo" to the waves. They crash into her, soaking her legs, almost pulling her under. Jonah and Avram follow her in. The three emerge together, Jonah in my mother's arms and Avram, under her watchful eyes, wet and grinning.

Ben and I, shaking our heads, sit on a piece of driftwood on the beach and, enjoying a quiet moment together, watch the beautiful spectacle that is our family. Then we join them in the surf, where we play until the sky turns golden-red. Our hungry stomachs pull us into a casual seafront restaurant, where we dine on freshly caught fish, shrimp, and clam chowder.

The next morning, being thoroughly spent, I would sleep in if left to my own devices. But Mom has other ideas. She wakes us just after sunrise to explore the wild and wonderous Oregon beach while the tide is at its lowest. Though early summer, it is cold. We head down to the beach in our winter coats. The water is frigid but the tide pools, brimming with treasures, beckon us.

Mom collects sea vegetables: long thick kombu, pointy kelp fronds, and translucent nori. Putting them in large plastic bags, she will bring them back to the hotel room and string them up on a clothesline, where, while they dry and during our five-hour drive home, their stench will provide endless fodder for light-hearted teasing. Months later, the moisture and fishy smell having long since evaporated, we will add them to soups, our bodies appreciating their many benefits. Sea vegetables are said to contain virtually all of the minerals found in the ocean—the same minerals that pulse through our blood.

As the tide rises, we abandon our winter coats. Jonah, as usual, sheds *all* of his clothes and, with a giant grin on his face and penis flapping in the wind, runs along the shore flying a kite with (fully clothed) Ben and Avram beside him.

Mom stands facing the ocean, her arms outstretched, beaming.

I sit on a piece of driftwood, hands on my belly, and think of the tiny embryo growing in the ocean inside of me. I watch the waves. They are relatively calm now, but I know how violent and scary they can be. *Please let me manage the contractions. Please don't let them cut me.*

When we return home, morning sickness, like an unwanted repeat visitor, is waiting for me. I stop eating, but the puke keeps coming. This sucks. I really need someone to fuss over me. But Ben is not a fusser, and Laura is still gone.

The sweet "welcome baby" moments disappear. Every day the scale confirms that I've lost weight. *I don't want to be pregnant; my body so can't do this right now.* All I want to do is lie in the fetal position and puke. Exercise is out of the question. So are prenatal vitamins. *This was a dumb idea. I should have taken the stupid Plan B pills.* I know I need help, but I don't want to leave my home. Who am I kidding? I don't want to leave my bed.

The boys tear the house apart: hurricanes leaving paths of destruction in their wake. I don't care, as long as they don't jump on me or talk to me or touch me or (ow) nurse me. My nummies, having been nursed on for almost four years without a vacation (the last year by two children at once), no longer want to be touched, much less sucked on. I wean both boys. Without ceremony or excuse I simply refuse to nurse them.

When I first see the spotting, I don't care. I had spotted early in my first two pregnancies also. But the next day there is more blood. Lots more than there should be. I would be scared if I wasn't so sick. I call to talk to Dr. Vikson, but a nurse intercepts my call to say that, if I want to, I can come in so they can see if there is a "viable fetus."

Having learned my lesson during the first labor, I ask: "If there is a problem, can you do anything about it?"

"No. There's nothing we can do"

The baby is dead or it's not. This is a relief because it means getting out of bed won't make a difference. I opt to stay in bed.

The bleeding gets better over the next couple of days. Then it gets worse, sometimes soaking through multiple pads a day. Though the bleeding comes and goes, the morning sickness does not, so I stay in bed for three weeks until it's time to pull myself together for that appointment I had thoughtlessly agreed to with Dr. Vikson's receptionist. I am going alone, something I would not have done during the first two pregnancies, but Ben has the kids and their commotion is not conducive to calming the wild uprising in my belly.

First, I christen the waiting room with vomit. Feeling better, I'm somewhat present in the examining room when Dr. Vikson, remembering that I prefer fetoscopes, asks my permission before pulling out a Doppler to listen for a heartbeat.

Lying on the table, my belly exposed, I wish Ben were with me. Dr. Vikson squirts blue gel on my stomach. It's cold. Pressing the Doppler down firmly, she slowly moves it around my belly. I hear my pulse and my empty stomach gurgling but I don't hear a heartbeat. I look in her eyes for an answer. She shakes her head no. She can't find it.

"I would like to do an ultrasound?" It is a question. She is waiting for my approval.

A lump in my throat, I nod.

Not wanting to make eye contact with her, I look up at the white ceiling and again wish Ben was with me. *Maybe I'm not pregnant.* And for the first time since the morning sickness kicked in—clearly and without a doubt, even if I end up with another cesarean—I want this baby. I mean, I really want it. I pray. *Please, baby, you will like it with us. I'm sorry it took me a while to adjust to the idea of having you. Please don't leave, baby.*

The nurse wheels in a large machine. It makes a loud humming noise. More blue goop is slathered on my belly. I watch the small screen, not sure what I'm looking for but needing to try. My other ultrasounds had been at the very end of my pregnancies, when the baby's body was too big to fit in its entirety on the screen. To my inexperienced eye, those images didn't resemble a baby at all. But, unmistakably, I see this one! The head, arms, butt, and legs are all kicking and wiggling about! "That's it!" I exclaim, amazed that my baby is alive and that I can see it.

Dr. Vikson's hand hesitates just a moment. I can tell that she would like to do a complete ultrasound, but instead she removes the machine and smiles broadly at me.

My baby is alive!

After the exam is over and I've gotten dressed, Dr. Vikson, who had left the room, returns. She sits on one of the exam room chairs and invites me to sit on another. "We need to talk about the delivery," she says. "VBAC is no longer encouraged. A thirty-minute 'decision to incision' time used to be acceptable, but now, because of new ACOG guidelines, the hospital requires that we be able to operate immediately."

She waits for me to nod before continuing.

"To attempt a VBAC, the operating team must be in the hospital and ready while you labor. They cannot be doing anything else. An operating room also needs to be available."

She doesn't need to tell me that this doesn't make good business sense. It would be much easier for the hospital to just schedule a repeat cesarean.

"How much will it cost for the operating team to hang around?" I ask.

"Fifteen hundred dollars."

"Insurance won't cover it, will they?

She shakes her head. "No."

"How long will I be allowed to labor?" I ask, thinking of my previous multiple-day labors.

"They won't limit your time in labor, but they also won't reschedule other surgeries to keep the operating room open. If surgeries are scheduled while you are in labor, they will cancel them and require an immediate cesarean."

I want to argue, but there is no one to argue with. I sense that Dr. Vikson doesn't agree with this policy, that it binds her hands just as she must tie mine to the operating table. But I'm not certain; she is difficult to read.

I imagine myself trying to relax and birth in the hospital while, in the next room, a surgical team sits around all scrubbed up waiting for twelve or more hours "just in case." *Yeah, right.*

The hospital's new rules are based on studies showing an increase in uterine rupture. Though it's clearly on the rise, nobody knows why. An obvious-to-me culprit could be Cytotec, which is known to cause uterine rupture.[1] Hospitals are "fixing" the problem by not allowing VBACs. This strategy increases their profits,[2] makes scheduling easier, and prevents litigation.

But just because a cesarean would be good for the hospital doesn't mean it's good for me. If uterine rupture were the only possible complication, perhaps it would be. But on the whole, a vaginal birth is safer than cesarean. So, if I'm afraid of uterine rupture, I should schedule a repeat cesarean. But if I want to stay alive, I'm better off with a vaginal birth. And the odds of having a normal birth increase the farther I am from that room full of surgeons, all scrubbed up and ready to cut.

Dr. Vikson watches me quietly while I process this.

"Fine, I'll just labor at home with a midwife and come in when we know the schedule is open."

"Roanna, I'm sorry. If you work with a midwife, I am not allowed to take you on as a client. Hospital policy forbids it."

Though I know the answer already, I ask about other hospitals' policies.

"Other than us, no hospital in the area allows VBAC under any circumstances."

This hospital, this woman, is my only chance at a natural hospital birth. The odds are outrageous. I nod, visibly agreeing to submit to their rules. But my eyes and my heart beg her forgiveness for the lie that I will not use a midwife.

10 Eve's Truth

During the first two pregnancies I had been so confident, so certain of myself and of birth. I thought I could laugh at fear. I was sure I could dismiss the notion that birth is painful and difficult, a punishment even—an idea as old as the beginning of time. According to Genesis 3:16, Eve sinned by eating a forbidden apple in the Garden of Eden, and God said, "I will greatly multiply your pain in childbirth, in pain you will bring forth children; yet your desire will be for your husband, and he will rule over you."

And even though I did find labor to be painful, I refuse to believe that it's supposed to be, or that God would be so offended about Eve's eating an apple that he would take it out on all women for the rest of time. Nope, I don't like it at all. I'm not interested in pain in childbirth or being ruled by my husband either.

Determined to upend this myth, I ask the local rabbi (and father of an incredible midwife), David Zaslow, about this story. He provides an alternative translation.

"Adam blames Eve. Eve blames nature, in the form of the snake. Both have fallen into dualistic thinking. And both Eve and Adam receive consequences for their *blame*. But these are not permanent consequences. When we love our bodies and treat them well; when we love the earth and treat it properly; when we stop lying to each other and to the Divine; when the Divine calls and we say *hinayni* (here I am) and we stop hiding from our higher selves; when the Divine asks 'What did you do?' and we answer honestly, even if we have to say 'I am sorry' instead of blaming others, then childbirth is fluid. Then the work is not laborious for both men and women."

What is it I that have blamed others for and been dishonest about?

Finally, six weeks pass and Laura returns and agrees to meet with me. Waiting for her while putting on beans to soak and chopping vegetables in my kitchen, I see her forest green Subaru pull up to the house only a moment late, as usual. Also as usual, she sits in her car for another five to ten minutes while she finishes a phone call, presumably with another client.

Watching her nod sympathetically to the voice on the phone, my mind wanders to how the new VBAC policies affect not only hospitals but trickle down to midwives as well. Liability insurance is expensive. Hospitals shift this expense onto the patient's health insurance, but midwives don't have that luxury. Few insurance companies cover home birth midwifery care. Most clients pay for home births out of their own pockets. This puts midwives in the horrible position of having to choose between practicing without insurance and not practicing at all.

Even if Laura agrees with me and believes that the new uterine rupture studies are flawed because they lump women who were given Cytotec together with women who were not, even if she simply believes that because it's my body it's my choice, in today's litigious society, it's a risk for her to take on a VBAC client.

While usually the midwife's role is to encourage the pregnant woman, helping her find her power, her belief in herself and in her body, I fear that in my case the roles are reversed. I must convince Laura that I am strong, that I am worth the risk.

I greet Laura at the door, and we sit together on the couch. She is tall with curly thick dark hair except for a single thick streak of white on the front left. She doesn't wear makeup but adorns herself with scarves and a generous amount of silver jewelry: earrings, pins, a small snake ring. Bangles with tribal patterns hang from her wrists. She tends to wear soft, silky and velvet clothing, making me want to reach out and pet her, to rub against her like a cat and curl up in her lap.

Looking down at my own daily uniform—a wrinkled T-shirt, jeans, and sneakers—I feel woefully inadequate. Laura obliges me with a hug. Looking into her eyes, I see that my own reflection is beautiful there.

As with all truly gorgeous people, Laura's spirit is not contained in her body. It seeps out through her pores, her deep laugh scattering it around the room. But I'm getting ahead of myself. She is not laughing yet. As I expected, she is understandably hesitant about taking me on as a client. In addition to the current climate of fear around allowing a trial of labor after a previous cesarean, her experience during my last pregnancy (her first and only attempted VBAC) was not positive. She tells me that Diane Vikson, whom she holds in great respect and has an ongoing professional relationship with, was upset with her and Laureen for "allowing" me to wait so long before I transported to the hospital.

Laura asks: "Why do you think you would be able to give birth this time? What's different?"

"I don't know. Tell me what to do. I will do anything and everything."

She waits. Her hesitancy hangs between us like a thick blanket.

"I don't want to be cut open. I must try."

"I want it for you, Roanna. But last time your obsession with having a VBAC compromised your well-being and Jonah's. I cannot commit to a home birth with you. If you want me to, I will work with you through the pregnancy. With the support of a second fully qualified midwife—Rhione has agreed, if you are willing—as well as my assistant, Veege, I will support you in early labor at home, but we will have to wait and see about the delivery."

I could call other midwives until I find one who isn't concerned about my history. But if I can get Laura to believe in me, then maybe I can believe in myself.

I nod, accepting her offer to work with me while my words repeat her promise to not automatically deny me. "I don't need the promise of a home birth. I just want you to allow for the possibility."

The following week, during our first official prenatal appointment, Laura asks, "How are you feeling?"

"Good. I'm glad the morning sickness is gone," I reply.

She is quiet, clearly waiting for me to say more. I shoot her a confident smile instead.

"How do you feel about being pregnant?" she persists.

"Great."

"Mmm-hmmm," she says, inviting more.

What does she want from me? "I'm hoping for a girl this time."

"Why is that?"

"Just because there is enough testosterone happening in this house already!"

"Mmmm-hmmm," Laura says, nodding and waiting.

What the hell is she waiting for? What does it matter? It will be a boy or it will be a girl. I have no control over it. Meanwhile, she sits there completely attentive as if she is listening to me, even though I'm not saying a thing. And, because I can't think of anything else to say, I end up telling her about the Orgasmic Amazon Queen Sex and my dreams of pink, lacy, baby girl clothing.

This she finds fascinating. She wants me to articulate the difference I feel carrying a girl instead of a boy, as if I can really tell if I am carrying a girl. She seems to think my intuition is interesting and important. This unnerves me, but I've promised to do what she says, so I ignore the tears that threaten and answer every one of her questions.

I meet with Rhione and Veege only once, but Laura comes every week. Each appointment lasts two hours. If she charged by the hour, this baby would cost as much as my uninsured cesarean. Our conversations are not limited to birth. Together we explore my other baggage: my relationship with my parents, my suicide attempt, friendships, and sexual history. She pries into my thoughts, fears, feelings and emotions, things that, in my opinion, are best left alone. "Let's talk about strengthening exercises and foul things I can eat or drink to ready myself for the battle of birth. I've always wanted to walk on fire."

"Emotions are your battle, Roanna," she says. "Toughness is just a reflection of weakness. Tears are the path to strength."

When Laura asks a painful question, my throat literally constricts, resisting the expression of my feelings and thoughts. But Laura's no dummy. She smiles and laughs until the jokes and diversions—my first layer of defense—pass. Then she sits silently, holding my eyes in hers. We are alone with the question. Clumsily, I put words to the previously unacknowledged demons rolling around inside of me. She sits and, without breaking eye contact, nods. She is silent except for the occasional "mmm-hmmm." That sound alone brings me to tears. It means I'm to go deeper. It means another layer has to be peeled off, exposing the rawness underneath. It means that my story must change.

"You're doing great, Roanna. This is your work. To open your body, you must first open your soul."

Laura believes that women often labor and birth the same way they were born, that our bodies remember and repeat our own birth experience. I think of what my friend Kristine shared with me: Certain of the day she conceived and three weeks past her calculated due date, she expressed concern to her mother. "I don't know what the big deal is," her mom replied, "you were born four weeks late." Sure enough, both of Kristine's children were born right "on time": three weeks and five days after their official due dates.

Though I want to dismiss this as coincidence, I am in no position to argue. I myself was born two weeks late by cesarean, just like my boys. When I ask my mom about it, she tells me my birth story, as she has many times before. But this time I listen. After I, her first baby, was delivered, the doctor told my mother that she would never be able to birth vaginally. Not wanting a repeat cesarean or the five-day separation from her baby that resulted from a botched surgery, when she became pregnant with my brother Orin, she asked a Chinese herbalist for help. He gave her a special "female" white ginseng root. As instructed, she placed the ginseng, with water, inside a small, sealed crock and cooked it (the same root over and over again) one hour every day for the thirty days before my brother was due, finally drinking the liquid when she went into labor.

Her labor went so quickly that though the staff tried to prepare for a cesarean, they didn't have enough time. My brother was born, peeing in the doctor's face, before they had the chance to anesthetize her.

Mom promises to find this rare kind of ginseng and brew this special tea for me. "Thank you," I say, feeling my eyes smart. *What is Laura doing to me? My emotions are out of control.*

One afternoon five months into the pregnancy, I happen to see an article in Ashland's local newspaper about an intuitive psychotherapist from Australia, Elizabeth Robinson, who has recently started a practice here in town. I'm immediately intrigued. The article says she "works with spirit guides and angels." It also says she has a degree in professional counseling. *I don't need therapy but maybe "spirit guides and angels" can fix me. I've already left logic behind. Why not try some magic?*

Elizabeth's office is nothing like what I had envisioned. There are no capes, crystal balls, or mystical accoutrements to be seen. She is about forty, petite and attractive, and is wearing black slacks and a pressed pale blue blouse. She strikes me as being light, but not in the sense of either underweight or flighty. It's more as if gravity doesn't pull as hard on her as it does on the rest of us. With a delightful Australian accent and a twinkle in her eye, she greets me.

"Hello," she says to me. "And hello to you, you gorgeous little bunny," she says, smiling at my belly. "She's responding to me. I can hear her making sounds—but with her mind."

"She!" She said "she!" I smile back, liking Elizabeth immediately for this alone.

"What beautiful eyes! The soul connection between you two is very strong. She is coming into your life as a teacher, but the lessons are special ones. The two of you are very close—a very warm and precious connection."

I want to believe her. She doesn't seem the slightest bit cuckoo except that she regularly pauses to listen to people I can neither hear nor see.

I tell Elizabeth about tearing a hole in my uterus and how I want to have a natural birth.

"Just let me tune in, then." She holds her hands up and apart while rubbing her fingertips together, as if, like a snake, she can taste the air with them. "Oh yes. That's right," she says as she nods, her eyes closed. "I see you in another lifetime. Your life was ended by a wound to the stomach. I can see a man, and I can feel not only that he ends your life with a dagger of some sort, but as he does, he holds an intense dislike for you, which was also absorbed into your body. Your body still holds that memory from the experience."

While she works her fingertips, her face contracts. Her brows raise and a breathy sound escapes her lips: "ooowhhhh," as if expelling something horrible. She appears to be in pain.

Is she pretending? How could she know this?

"This man who ended your life intensely believed that you had absolutely no value." Her fingers pause. Her eyes open now, she stares at my stomach. Tilting her head to the right, she leans in really close, close enough that I hope I'm wearing clean panties. She seems to be looking past my clothing and skin and into my belly. Now she tilts her head to the left.

"Ah, I see. The knife is still in there. The pain of it is still there," she says, touching the place on my incision where the sharp pains still come.

I nod, agreeing to the pain while withholding judgment about the knife.

"Okay. We are going to take this out."

And she does. At least, her hand grabs hold of something and pulls on it with such conviction that I find myself surprised when I don't see a knife emerge from my body.

Shaking her hands as if to air dry them, she declares the task done. And just like that, the twinges stop completely. I've never had another one.

While telling Ben about the session, I hear a touch of skepticism in my voice. When it was happening it all seemed so real, but outside her office, surrounded by people who don't hear voices, my doubts resurface.

"Do you think it was real?" Ben asks.

Am I gullible? Am I wasting money? How do I know she's really psychic and not just crazy? "After three and a half years of consistent twinges, the pain is gone," I reply, choosing to avoid both my own and Ben's questions.

Yet I wonder: If she can do that, maybe she can help me give birth. So I visit her again. "Please help me have a natural birth."

"I can't create your future for you," Elizabeth replies. "I can only help you see what you are holding within yourself that keeps you from having what you want."

"I'm not sabotaging this," I snort. "I want a natural birth more than anything."

"So many women I've worked with carry resistance to being a mother or giving birth. They absolutely consciously desire it, but on some deeper level their bodies carry another, unacknowledged story that manifests the opposite."

"Please just try," I say, certain that I have no resistance to having a baby and that she will see this once she starts rubbing her fingertips together.

Leaning forward, an indulgent but not unkind look to her face, Elizabeth nods almost imperceptibility. Her eyes close, and her hands separate. As she rubs her fingertips, her words flow quickly. "I'm being shown a thick gray layer of old emotional debris right across the neck of your cervix. It's full of sadness and fear. It's like a plug stopping the babies from passing through.

"It's two centuries ago, or even the early 1700s. There is a large four-poster bed, blood on the sheets. A maid is attending you. There are layers of heavy blankets, drapes, and white-capped women are close by. Your nightgown is on, and you are in intense pain. The association with the blood, the mess, the baby, and your life as a mother is one of sadness. You are having to let go of so many things in life that you really want.

"I sense you are quite young and the man you are married to is older, someone you don't really want to be with much. You fulfilled expectations in marrying him. Your job is to produce an heir, but you want to see the world and to experience life beyond the roles of wife and mother. Giving birth means giving up your dreams.'"

Could I have ever not wanted a baby? I try to imagine being married to a man I don't like and being pregnant for the sole purpose of producing an heir. *A natural birth has been my focus for so long. Is there more to me than this?*

"There are others moving forward in spirit now to assist." Elizabeth's brow lifts and her lips soften to a smile, as if greeting the dearest of friends. She raises her right hand palm and points behind my right shoulder. "Beings of light. They are moving in toward you now to assist in your healing."

Though I can't see them any more than I saw the invisible knife leave my body, the room definitely gets swooshy. I feel like I'm going to faint but can't remember how to get my head all the way down between my legs to stop it.

Elizabeth keeps talking. I hear the words, but even though I recognize them to be English, they don't make any sense to me.

Opening my mouth to ask what's happening, I find I've forgotten how to speak. Tremendous pressure bears down upon the top of my head, pushing it deep into my shoulders. The pressure moves down, comes around my head, moving clockwise as it drops—or does my head turn into it? As suddenly as it started, the pressure completes a counterclockwise sweep and is gone. The swooshyness ends.

Words keep flowing from Elizabeth's mouth, but I still can't understand them. It's as if the left side of my brain has shut off. I don't remember going home. Though it's the middle of summer, I awake late in the afternoon to find myself curled into the fetal position deep in heavy blankets on my bed.

In the morning, purified from an evening of sobbing and a good night's sleep, I try to explain what happened to Laura: "It wasn't painful but it was really intense. My head felt like it was being squished. I would say that my head went through a birth canal, except for the strange turning."

Vaulting from the couch, Laura takes, from her bottomless woven basket, a skeleton model of a woman's pelvis and, from the floor, Avram's multi-colored plush toy bunny. Excitedly, she says, "But the baby's head does turn in the birth canal!" Pushing the bunny's head into the skeletal pelvis, she continues: "A baby begins sideways, with its back along the mama's left hip. As the baby moves down, the mother feels pressure in her bowels. Sometimes it feels as if the baby is going to come out through the anus. Really. Then when the baby maneuvers through the pubic arch, it turns left to face the mother's back in order to fit, and then right as its body emerges! The baby turns 45 degrees, twice, just like you felt!"

Oh wow. I had always focused so much on what my body was doing during labor, that I had never stopped to think about the baby's experience.

Laughing, I grin at Laura. "Maybe Elizabeth's magic is real!" And to myself, for I'm not ready to say it aloud: *Maybe my intuition is real.*

Willing to further explore the emotional aspect of birth, I read *Birthing from Within* by Pam England, a book my mom gifted to me when I was pregnant with Avram. I didn't read it back then, figuring that I (being superior and all) didn't need to prepare for birth; I would just tough it out. That was a different me, a different life. Here I am, exploring my emotions and intuitive stuff and crying. *I must really be carrying a girl.*

Birthing from Within suggests that I draw pictures of my baby and my births. Believing that they will only ever be seen by me, I draw quickly, carelessly. First I draw labor:

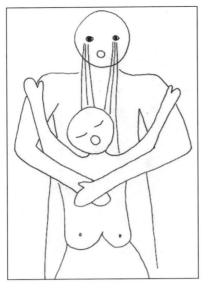

My eyes are closed because I'm so inward. My mouth is open as I breathe through a contraction. Ben is huge and strong and holding me. His beautiful blue eyes are not confined to their sockets but reach down to me. He is completely present.

Next I draw Avram's delivery:

The rat-like thing on the floor is the placenta, which they tossed out in a "hazardous waste" receptacle. My upper body is completely separated from the lower. The doctor is the only one with eyes or detail or power, her face and mask are skeletal-looking. Except for the blood dripping from my belly, there is nothing to me. I don't matter. The only warmth in this picture is the light shining around Ben and Avram.

Finally I draw my children, and my baby as I imagine her to be in utero.

Light surrounds my three children. Drawn before the birth, the baby's eyes are brown, while my boys have hazel-green eyes, just like in real life.

While I am drawing the third picture something in me shifts. I see, this time by my own colored pencils, that the most important thing is that my children are happy, healthy, and connected. Though I have always *said* that a healthy baby is the most important outcome, in truth I have been so obsessed with the VBAC that I haven't valued much else. Tears in my eyes, I talk to the baby in the picture, the baby in my womb. *If we have to go through a cesarean, it will be okay. Birth is not everything. We have an entire lifetime to share.*

But this acceptance of the unknown does not mean I will agree to an unnecessary cesarean. With a vengeance, I continue to train for a natural birth, revisiting many of the alternative practitioners I saw during my second pregnancy.

"Eat bone stock," Max says, "to increase your chi."

Dutifully I purchase packages of "dog bones" from Ashland's natural food co-op, simmering them overnight with water and a bit of vinegar. In the morning, I am rewarded with a pot full of grizzle and unidentifiable spongy stuff floating on top of a brownish concentrate, all covered in a thick layer of grease and cappuccino-like brown and white foam. The house smells exactly like the stuff looks.

Thankfully, Ben handles the next part. As he pours the stock through a strainer into storage containers, bone steam rises, filling his nose and moistening his face. As the stock cools, he digs into the larger bones with a chopstick, working out bits of marrow to eat. Then he sucks out whatever remaining marrow juices he can from the bones, slurping all the while and laughing at the look of repulsion on my face.

I store the bone stock in the refrigerator, where it turns into a gelatinous mass, resembling what you would get if you mixed milk chocolate Jell-O with whipped cream. This concoction I add to almost everything I make, substituting it for a bit of the water. Thankfully, it tastes better than it looks, adding a rich and somewhat gamey flavor to our food.

The herbalist tells me I am not to eat dairy, sugar, coffee or chocolate, and to allow myself only a little fruit. I quit them all, even the chocolate. At home it's easy to restrict my diet this way, but when I am working in the restaurant, I am surrounded by sugar and espresso and all things sweet and delectable: mochas, chai lattes, lemon basil cookies, lavender cake, goji berry cookies, chocolate panini with white chocolate whipped cream, and rose lemonade. Every time I take a batch of cookies from the oven, I contemplate taking just a nibble. But weighed against the regret I would feel if I end up with another cesarean, it's just not worth it.

Do I really think that one little bite of cookie will make the difference? No, but if I end up with another cesarean, I need to know that it was not from lack of effort. So, instead of fresh dragon's breath ginger cake, I eat garlic and chipotle chicken soup. It is delicious, but it's not dragon's breath ginger cake.

Late one night, longing for a treat, I wander the aisles of the co-op, looking forlornly at the rows of chocolate cookies, cakes, pies, chips, and ice cream. Whining to myself, I buy an unfamiliar fruit instead. It's a squat, pumpkin-looking thing about the size of a tomato. I didn't know it would be the most luscious fruit ever. Its flavor is deep and complex, its texture soft and slippery, almost sensual. *How have I gone through life not knowing about this?* I think to myself, consuming yet another persimmon.

Remembering how Hypnobirthing helped me stay calm during labor with Jonah, especially during hospital transport, I decide to try hypnotherapy. I lie on a couch, listening to the therapist, who, in a sing-song voice, counts me into a state of half-sleep, one where lead runs through my veins and talking is a burden. Prodding around in this part-dream, part-memory place, she digs deep into my subconscious. She brings me back to Avram's and Jonah's cesareans, asking me to recount them. I do, surprised as I speak to find that, though there is still sadness, the "charge" is gone. I finally seem to be arriving at a place of acceptance.

Then there is exercise. I jog three miles a day every day, seven days a week: no exceptions. Have I mentioned that I hate to exercise? I do. I really do. But that's irrelevant.

Raw milk is Stella's recommended elixir. According to her, it contains vitamins, enzymes, and all twenty-two essential amino acids. Referring to the pasteurization process, she says, "Which would you rather eat, a carrot that was heated to 275 degrees two months ago or a fresh one?" She has a point. The herbalist who told me not to eat dairy agrees, adding that many people who are allergic to pasteurized milk products have no reactions to raw ones.

Looking online, I discover an entire raw milk movement, a controversial one that the American Dairy Association claims is dangerous. As a business person, I can see that pasteurization is a no-brainer. It extends product life by two months, preventing waste, and using the pasteurization process to "purify" dirty and infected milk. As a consumer and a parent of children who enjoy dairy, I want raw milk.

Raw milk can't be bought in a store. The sale of it borders on illegal in most states. In Oregon it's okay to sell it as "pet food" (wink, wink), but even then it's hard to find. The easier alternative is to buy a cow. After all, there are no laws against drinking milk from your own cow, only against selling it. By contracting with a farmer, one can buy a share of a cow and the milk it produces. Of course, one must pay the farmer seven dollars a gallon to care for the cow.

The closest cow I can find to share is Buttercup. She lives forty-five minutes away in the town of Rogue River. Unfortunately, seven dollars a gallon doesn't include delivery, so a small group of raw milk believers and I take turns once a week driving out to pick up and deliver gallons of this fresh medicine. The boys and I skim cream from the top, blending it in the Cuisinart until it turns into butter. The remaining milk we experiment with, drinking some raw and salting the rest into cheese so fresh that it squeaks in our teeth.

In addition to milk, I drink lots of water, but not before, during, or after eating. It would dilute the digestive enzymes.

Meanwhile, Laura instructs: "Talk to the baby. Ask her to get in the right position. Visualize her moving down the birth canal." Probably as a trick to get me to sit long enough to visualize, she tells me I must take foot baths for fifteen minutes every day.

I visit an energy healer, Dianne. On a stone at her entry way, sitting next to some used-to-be cowgirl boots, now flower planters, the words "On the other side of fear, you will always find freedom" are written. As I lie on a massage table, Dianne wraps me in warm towels and works scented oils into my skin. I fall asleep with her hands resting softly on my body.

Forty minutes later, I awake to find her smiling at me.

"The council came and, wrapping you in golden cords, rocked your body like a hammock. They dipped you into dazzling darkness and your twelve-pointed star shone brightly," she tells me.

I nod, not from understanding but because I feel even better than after a deep-tissue massage. Smiling, I sign up for another appointment.

The supplements I take are almost a meal in themselves. There is acidophilus, foul-tasting brown liquid for iron, organic beef liver pills from New Zealand (the New Zealand part is important: fewer chemicals), and of course prenatals, enzymes, and vitamins B and C and others that I can't even remember—handfuls of pills, three times a day.

Between Pangea, my two demanding boys, and all of the physical and emotional work involved in preparing for this birth, I rarely stop to think about the actual baby who will be born to us, making ours a family of five. It is Jonah, barely a year and a half old, who seems most connected to this little soul. Multiple times a day he lifts my shirt just to kiss my belly and say "hi baby."

He's just a baby himself. How will he feel when his position on my lap is stolen away by a sucking, screaming, poopy newborn? Will he still welcome the baby?

In addition to seeing Laura, the hypnotist, herbalist, psychic, Max the mad scientist, an acupuncturist, and a homeopath, I continue to see Dr. Vikson regularly. During our brief, twenty-minute appointments, I tell her about all of the alternative things I am doing and ask what more I can do to improve my chances of a vaginal birth. She tells me that she thinks there is a complication with my placenta and reminds me of the dangers involved. But she doesn't point to any test telling her so. It's as if she also, even though she's a doctor, is working from intuition.

It's heartbreaking. I have come to really respect her. I so desire her blessing for a VBAC, as if her giving it would make me worthy of natural birth. Yet the process I am in is not just about birth. A battle is going on inside of me, a battle of science against trust, of using my own strength against surrendering to another's power over me, of my dominant masculine, left brain against my feminine, right brain, which, until now, I believed was lesser-than.

"I am willing to accept a cesarean if it's necessary. I simply can't accept that it is without trying," I protest.

But knowing that a trial of labor depends on the operating schedule, she cannot promise me one. She tells me stories about other cesareans, about women who, for various reasons, recognized and accepted that a cesarean was actually the best thing for them and their babies. "You are still a woman and a mother, even if you don't achieve a natural birth," she tells me.

Is she absolving me from my past cesareans or preparing me for a future one?

Rationally, my mind understands. It believes her, even. But my heart does not. When I close my eyes, I hear it beat: "VBAC, VBAC, VBAC. . . ." My soul craves natural birth the way a lover's very being calls to her mate.

11 She Returns

The rain has returned and leaves are falling from the trees. The dark comes early now and nights are chilly, closing in on me. But it feels all wrong. It should be spring. Inside of me, something is stirring. I can't place it.

Ben and I have been in Ashland seven wonderful years. Pangea is successful. I have two fabulous boys and a strong marriage. It's the perfect life, the exact one I wished for. Yet without these—the roles of boss, business owner, wife, and mother—what is left that's me? What if, like coats, I shed all of these labels? Who would be left?

As if searching for the answer online, sitting at my computer I follow the links from one website to another, ending up on a site brimming with winged creatures, shell-bound elfin folk, and long-necked goddesses, all hand sculpted by fantasy doll artist Marilyn Radzat. *The boys would love these.* But these figures are not toys. They are works of art purchased by people with pockets much deeper than mine including Demi Moore, Anne Rice, Ron Howard, and the former President and Mrs. Clinton.

On one page a photo of Marilyn on a sunny beach comes up. It's been formatted like an invitation, welcoming me to join her and her friend and fellow doll artist, Gail Lackey, in Hawaii for an art doll retreat. *I want to go.* Book-marking the site, I add it to my "Someday List."

My Someday List is full of things that will happen when I have more money or time or. . . .

"Who are you kidding?" my inner child demands, attacking me. "Your Someday List is where you stuff your dreams. When you're not feeling your best, you pull them out and use someday to dull the pain of now."

Ouch. My inner child is a pain in the ass. The truth is, I do have the time and money, but going to Hawaii alone lies outside my comfort zone. *Why is that? I've traveled on my own before, backpacking through Europe when I was twenty-one.* But that was long ago, before Ben and marriage and boys. I haven't been apart from them for more than a few nights. *What happened to me?*

The intuitive therapist Elizabeth's smile comes suddenly to mind. *Am I remembering her, or is she here?* She is saying ". . . you want to see the world and to experience your life beyond the roles of mother and wife."

But I'm so busy. It's easier just to stay here.

My eyes fall on Marilyn's promise shining out at me from the computer screen: "I believe in Enchantment in her highest form. Not as an escape from reality, but as a window into what is possible."

Maybe it is possible. Maybe I could just go. Maybe it could be that simple.

Half hoping he will say no, I ask Ben what he thinks. After all, I can't force him to watch the boys for ten days. If he doesn't want to, I will have to stay home and there will be a good reason for the death of this particular "someday." Besides, I don't know how to make art.

But Ben is not that kind of husband. He says, "Go. It is money well spent. I will take care of the boys. Have a great time." There is no hesitancy in his voice.

Bastard.

In the grand scheme of things, I know it's not so bad if for a week the boys eat pizza every night, stay up late watching movies, and their clothes don't match. Ben is an attentive dad. The boys adore him and, even if he doesn't put them to sleep as early as I would, he holds them when they are sad or hurt, claps and high fives when they accomplish something new, and listens to them when they have a story to tell. So, even though I can't find a swimsuit that will cover my now gargantuan body, I leave the November rains in Oregon and fly to sunny Oahu.

At the Honolulu airport Marilyn and Gail greet me and the other participants, welcoming each of us warmly with a fresh creamy-yellow orchid lei. Looking around, I realize we are all women. *It's an art doll retreat, Roanna, of course it's all women. Why is this uncomfortable?* As we drive for an hour through pineapple fields towards the North Shore the women make small talk. I half listen but it's hard to focus through the chatter inside of my own head. It's judging them, nitpicking them, even. Though I don't approve of these thoughts, they keep coming. Marilyn tells me she thinks I am brave for coming all this way pregnant and alone, to which, with a shrug, I lie, "Oh, it's really no big deal."

The North Shore is the old haunting grounds of the Beach Boys and famous for its world-class waves. Though there are plenty of tourists, it is completely unpretentious. Board shorts and "slippas" are the attire of choice. Surfboards abound, strapped to the tops of cars or planted vertically in the ground, looking as much a part of the garden as the tropical flowers. Nobody seems to be rushing anywhere but down to the ocean. It's easy to slow down here. There is so much to see and enjoy.

We're housed in Marilyn's personal residence on a secluded private beach on Kawela Bay. Outside, a sign, posted next to a blue-green hammock overlooking the ocean, reads: "Heaven is a little closer in a cottage by the sea." Using her fantasy artist's eye, Marilyn has enchanted her home rather than decorating it. Little faces peek at me from under stones. Fairies dance on shelves. Giant wings, begging to be slipped on, hang on the wall. These expensive treasures do not reside behind glass but flirtingly invite me to pick them up, to play. Each has a story to tell, and each one includes some sort of secret chamber full of jewels or other treasures to discover. Marilyn's title, "curator of enchantment," is well earned. Magically, being in her house calls the little girl in me to the surface. I could spend my entire ten days here, doing nothing but exploring her home and be perfectly delighted.*

---

* To see pictures of Marilyn Radzat's enchanted home and studio, visit www.cutstapledandmended.com/bonus/.

In my room, a turquoise sarong with a batiked pattern of swimming dolphins is waiting for me. A handwritten card next to it invites me to leave my old clothing and self behind and join the others on the beach. Taking off my habitual uniform of jeans and T-shirt, I see that the sarong leaves my bra straps showing. So I take my bra off too. My breasts are fully supported by my large belly. All that's left is my underwear, so I take that off as well.

I wrap the sarong around my body and walk out the few steps from my room onto the secluded beach, where a Hawaiian woman, her long black hair contained in a crown of shells, is waiting. She reminds me of Laura. She is powerful but also feminine and beautiful. The circular tribal tattoo on her left shoulder would be considered trendy by any of my acquaintances, but there's nothing trendy about Pahia; she's the real thing. She is a *kahuna*, or Hawaiian priestess. It is her birthright, passed down through her maternal lineage.

Marilyn and Gail stand on either side of Pahia. The rest of us, ten women of varying shapes, sizes, and colors, complete the circle. As instructed, we each carry a slip of paper on which we have written what we are letting go of. Embarrassed by the chatter in my head on the drive up, mine says "judgment." I'm determined to let go of my judgment of these women-strangers who I'm to spend the next ten days with.

In a coconut bowl a small fire is lit. Without speaking, each woman drops her slip of paper into the fire. Wanting the ritual to touch me, I force my fingers into the fire to release my paper, to release my judgment of others.

The fire licks at my fingers. "It's your self-judgment you must shed, Roanna," it whisper-laughs back to me.

"Welcome. I have prepared a special healing tea for you," Pahia says as she pours piping hot tea into small cups for us. It tastes like the smell of fresh straw.

That evening, by candlelight, we are fed a fabulous homemade dinner, mine specially prepared with extra protein according to my pregnancy requirements by Patricia, an ocean-kayaking enthusiast with a beautiful and contagious donkey laugh. The women's conversation is light and friendly but I hold back. We come from worlds apart. I listen carefully, watching how these women get to know one another, asking each other questions and genuinely appreciating each others differences.

After dinner, we are presented with a chocolate haupia pie from Ted's Restaurant (a North Shore favorite). I, who have been so compulsive with my diet, relax and indulge in a small sliver of this incredible coconut-custard-chocolate-pudding pie, holding each bite reverently in my mouth as it melts to nothing.

It's late now, and our plates are whisked off, with all offers of help nicely but firmly rebuffed. We take flashlights and walk a few short steps down to the beach to visit with the giant sea turtles that have come up on the shore to sleep. The others dance in the tide under the indulgent eyes of the peaceful turtles. It looks fun, and though I'm not a dancer, I twirl a bit. Grinning, I try to remember the last time I stood outside under the stars for no reason other than to play in the ocean and visit with a four-legged creature.

The next morning I wake up curiously early: before the sun. The birds are already singing. I'm not sure what to do with myself. At home, my day begins as soon as I wake up, whether it's caring for the boys, starting into my to-do list, or getting ready to work in the restaurant. But this morning, I wrap a sarong around my otherwise naked body, drape the still-fresh lei around my neck, and walk along the beach.

My footprints are the only ones in the sand. Last night's dancing steps have long since washed away. The turtles are back in the water, their heads bobbing up to look about every so often. Heading to my right, I walk beyond the calm inlet sheltering Marilyn's house to where giant waves from the open sea crash down on the reef. How strange it is to be here, in this tropical paradise, while my family is fast asleep across the ocean. Finding a large rock, I sit and, serenaded by birds, watch the sky change color. While sitting quietly usually bores me, this sunrise is fully engaging. I am content to do nothing but give thanks for this moment and drink in the sensual beauty that is Hawaii.

As I walk back down the beach, small crabs with one ridiculously disproportionate large claw scurry away into holes in the sand. Pretty shells catch my eye. I resolve to bring along a gathering bag next time. There is no doubt in my mind that, even without an alarm clock, I will wake each morning to walk the beach and watch the sun rise.

Back at Marilyn's house, there is breakfast of hard-boiled eggs, granola, yogurt, scones hot from the oven, and fresh papaya. When I try to wash my dish, Patricia takes it from me and, shaking her head with a small "don't you dare" laugh, gestures outside, where the other women are sitting.

It would be easier to do the dishes, I think, feeling the judgmental chatter rising again in my head. *Why do these horrible thoughts keep coming? I'm not this kind of person.* But then I realize that I am. It's just that back home my judgments are more insidious. I've become so used to the people in my life that I don't actually think the judgments. They are simply there. Here, in a completely new situation, surrounded by only strangers and with nothing else to distract myself with, I am embarrassingly aware of them.

Why am I so judgmental?

I swear I can hear Laura say, "mmm-hmmm."

Oh crap. Here comes the emotional stuff. I make an excuse and head to the privacy of my room. No sooner do I close the door than it comes. *My judgments make other people appear less important and give me an excuse to distance myself from them.*

Wiping a hint of wet from my eyes, I look in the mirror and, shaking my head, raise my eyebrows at myself. *I can do this.*

When I return to the group, the judgment, having been called out, simply disappears. I see the women's faces, words, and expressions, and, instead of disregarding them, I encourage curiosity to grow. As if glimpsing my interactions from a different perspective, I see myself habitually diverting away from any topic that feels intimate. It's a tactic

I've used since childhood. But it does not bring me pleasure; it exhausts me. It bores me, even.

These women don't know anything about me. They don't know that I'm prickly and defensive. I could drop that identity and create an entirely new persona. I could be anybody—a CIA agent, CEO of a Fortune 500 company, even an author. But I don't want to go back to my room to put on panties, much less try think up a whole new person. Besides, I'll never see these women again. I don't have to impress them. Maybe I can just put down the armor and see what happens.

If I were home, this would be difficult, impossible even, because everyone—my employees and friends, Laura, my children, even my husband—expects me to be prickly and defensive. So I am. But I'm not home now.

Maybe it's the ocean's warm water lapping at my feet or the smell of the lei around my neck. It could be the fact that my responsibilities are three thousand miles away, or that there's not a man in sight. Maybe it's the lack of panties. Whatever it is, I'm astounded to see a soft and feminine creature emerge from me as easily as the hibiscus flower, moments ago at arm's length, ends up tucked behind my ear.

Each morning I wake to walk the beach and greet the rising sun, gathering the ocean's treasures along the way. After a shared breakfast with my new friends, we discover the wonders of the North Shore together. We explore ancient Hawaiian ceremonial grounds and walk through lush tropical gardens to a beautiful waterfall. One day we pass among giant banyan trees, exploring their many trunks, the vines thick enough to swing on. Another day we climb through old rusty barbed wire fencing to walk through miles of fields. Only horses and giant frogs are present to witness our delight as, on an otherwise deserted beach, we collect sea glass by the handful.

In the town of Haleiwa, we hit the boutiques, art galleries, and Matsumoto, a store selling shave ice (back home, people would say "snow cone"), where I indulge in my second treat: a colorful lychee–passion fruit shave ice with adzuki beans and ice cream hiding in the middle.

On the side of a long stretch of empty highway—past simple road-side stands offering bags of freshly cut mango, pineapple, and papaya, along with ice-cold coconuts, colorful straws sticking out of the top of each one—lie uniform small ponds: shrimp farms. Next to these are "shrimp shacks," which aren't really shacks at all but travel trailers with big "Shrimp" signs on them.

Being a restauranteur, I consider my title "food snob" well earned. While I don't eat fancy food every day, I only buy organic, have never eaten a TV dinner, and insist that food looks and tastes delicious. I would not, even with unbearable hunger pains, ever think to stop at a dilapidated trailer bearing the sign: "Fumi's Kahuku Shrimp. Harvest Daily. Live or Cooked. Live Shrimp Tank." But as part of the group, that's exactly where I find myself.

Sitting on a folding chair, plastic fork and paper towel napkin in hand, I eye the food in front of me. Two scoops of white rice, a slice of lemon, and unshelled shrimp sit in a pool of rough-chopped garlic and grease so deep that, in moments, it soaks both of the flimsy paper plates attempting to contain it.

Wanting to be a good sport, I tentatively take a small bite. . . . It is incredible. Abandoning the fork, I use both hands to release the shrimp from their shells and devour them. Pausing to breathe, I look up to see that there are more plates, each with a different kind of shrimp: coconut battered, hot and spicy, sweet and spicy, soy sauce, lemon butter shrimp, and more. Laughing, we pass plates back and forth to each other, each of us insisting that the plate we are handing off holds the best of them all. But in the end, after much negotiation, it is agreed that the garlic butter shrimp is the best.

"Shrimp Shack Shrimp" has since become a favorite Rosewood family dinner. Though it's not quite the same when made with anything other than shrimp caught only moments before, it's still really good.

Rosewood's Shrimp Shack Shrimp
Serves two

1 pound uncooked in-shell wild prawns
12 cloves garlic, enough to yield 4 TBL when rough-chopped
8 TBL butter
½ tsp red pepper flakes
1 ½ tsp salt

For serving:
2 cups cooked white rice
2 slices lemon
2 sprigs parsley

Peel and rough-chop the garlic. Sauté it in the butter and red pepper flakes until it begins to soften and brown slightly. Rinse the shrimp and add them to the pan with salt. Continue to sauté until the shrimp tighten in their shells and turn bright pink. Serve alongside rice, pouring excess garlic butter sauce onto the rice. Garnish with a lemon wedge and parsley.

While this is a lot easier to eat with shelled shrimp, it's authentic and more fun with unshelled shrimp.

Near the shrimp shack is an old antique and curio store. This truly is a shack, complete with a rickety porch and tilted roof. Inside, the shelves overflow with gaudy dye-colored shell bracelets, sarongs, old colored bottles, and antique costume jewelry. Assorted license plates adorn the walls.

But not everything inside is junk. Japanese fishing floats hang from the ceiling. Each of these blue-green orbs, the size and shape of my pregnant belly, was hand blown from recycled sake bottles. The tides have polished them to varying shades of iridescence as they traveled here from across the world. *How are they not broken by the waves?* I wonder, thinking of the intensity that is the ocean. Its push and pull reminds me of my own fragility in the face of the wave-like surges of birth. I select two of the bluest, most iridescent globes to send home, one for myself, and one for my mother.

Perhaps the North Shore is unpretentious because the ocean distracts from everything else. The waves here are enormous. Fifty feet enormous. People come from all over the world to ride them. And every year some, even experienced surfers, die trying.

Lifeguards, aware of the rogue waves that can grow up to three times larger than the rest, try to keep the sunburned tourists far enough back from the shore that even spray from the crashing waves doesn't reach them. Even so, onlookers push their bodies against the yellow "caution" tape, stretching it till the words distort. In spite of the dangers, the waves call all of us. Lifeguards, tourists, and locals alike are drawn to sit for hours, eyes riveted on the surf show. My new women friends and I, sitting shoulder to shoulder on beach blankets, "ohh," "ahh," and groan in unison as surfers catch or are crushed by waves. The lifeguards function also as coaches, using giant bullhorns to keep surfers from drifting too close to the rip tide and to coax the occasional panicking one back to shore.

When the lifeguards judge one beautifully built, black-haired male surf-worthy, allowing him to move past the yellow safety tape toward the sea, we stiffen in vicarious apprehension. How he will pass through the wall of white explosions where the waves hit the shore to get out to the giant cresting waves the surfers ride?

We watch as, seemingly unafraid, he runs straight into the action, his beaten-up yellow surfboard under his arm. I want to shout at him "Don't do it," but he dives down into and under the waves, popping out the other side. Smiling, he shakes his wet hair back from his eyes.

Why wasn't he pulverized? Again the wave-surge connection clicks in my mind. Could it be that underneath the violence of the contraction, there is a comfortable place to be?

In the afternoons, we work in the art studio. With the room's wall of sliding glass doors open to the beach, it feels like we are still outside.

At Marilyn's request, we bring something from nature every time we enter, placing it on a makeshift altar that soon fills with shells, flowers, gnarled driftwood, and other treasures.

In the center of the altar is a deck of goddess cards to shuffle and pick from. Every card offers a picture and insightful or inspiring words that seem perfect for the person who chose it. These we read aloud. It's almost impossible to not follow them with some comment about how they reflect the reader's life, which leads to questions and sharing.

Often the words coming out of my mouth are followed with the thought: *Did I really just say that?* Back home, even with those dearest and closest to me, I would have spoken only from my left brain, in a simple and emotion-free manner. Perhaps it's because I'm responding while simultaneously immersed in an art project that the right side of my brain seems to have been set free. I can actually feel it pulsing and engaging.

We have each been given a gourd as the base for our art project. It is hard to imagine that these bulbous, dried vegetables will become something beautiful, but Marilyn assures us she uses them in many of her fanciful creations. To the gourd we affix polymer clay. Though I haven't done this sort of thing before, it's not difficult. While the clay doesn't conform to what I intend, it also doesn't dry, so I can rework it till I'm content. I don't have a picture in mind of what I want to create, but I can tell when it is wrong and then ruthlessly tear it apart and rebuild it. I do this again and again, until it no longer feels as if I am creating something with the clay but rather that the clay is telling me something. If I just keep working at it, I might get it.

Baskets and boxes of treasures to use as we wish surround us. These aren't the sort that can be found in a craft store: handwritten pages from an 1882 French journal, a rusted vintage key, bridal netting from the turn of the century, handmade beads, abalone shells, yarn, golden thread, antique velvet, mirrors and jewels, plus paints, pigments, and brushes galore. I would work my piece day and night if Marilyn and

Gail didn't kick us out of the studio for some breathing space mid afternoon.

Though the rest of the North Shore is unswimmable this time of year, Marilyn's bay is protected by a reef that tames the giant waves. By the time they reach her house, a small child can safely swim in them. Banished from the art studio, we head to the bay, and once I am in a kayak, snorkeling next to a turtle, or just bobbing around in the ocean's splendor, I almost forget about my project.

But after dinner, when we have said goodnight to the turtles asleep on the beach, relaxed with a glass of wine (water for me), and the others have returned to their rooms to sleep or read, I sneak back to the studio and continue working on my piece. There is something I want to express, something that wants to come out of me. This clay is its voice.

The days pass quickly. I do not think of the restaurant or my to-do list. I do not even touch a computer. Every day my job is to take pleasure in being alive and to discover what this clay is telling me. Gradually it becomes something much more beautiful than I ever thought I could have made with my own inexperienced hands.

My gourd is pregnant. (How could she not be?) Her hands are on her belly, so immersed in what is happening inside that they melt, formless, into it. Her eyes are closed, but her face shines upward full of gratitude, bliss, and prayer. She is completely connected and fulfilled. She is not worrying about life or pondering the questions of the universe because somehow she knows.

Painting her a golden sheen, I tangle sea glass, shells, and other treasures I have collected from Hawaii's waters in her hair. On her back is a small hinge that opens to a bejeweled chamber, where I place a soft pillow made of vintage purple velvet on which lies a priceless gift: a small, rough black pebble.

Though the stone looks innocuous, thousands of pounds of these, often accompanied by notes of apology and addressed to "Queen Pele," are sent back to Hawaii each year. The senders—visitors who took home bits of this volcanic rock that Pele's curse forbids removing from Hawaii—are relieved to be rid of this object that created havoc in their lives. My little rock is different. Pahia, one of the few people who has the right to give away Pele's black treasure, gifted it to me.

When my pregnant gourd woman is finished, my ten days in Hawaii are over as well. Marilyn and Gail drive us back through the pineapple fields to the airport. Hawaii herself mourns our departure; showering us with tears, her sky fills with three full rainbows. The women I have spent ten days with will move on, never really knowing the transformation they gifted me with. In their wake, new women will come into my life. From now on, women-friends will be my anchor in the storm.

12 Ring of Fire

I arrive home to drawings and kisses and love. My children look older. It makes sense that they have changed; they have experienced life without their mom. I too have transformed, hardly feeling like the same person who left. I spent a whole ten days with me, someone who likes to watch the sunrise, turn strangers into meaningful friends, and create art.

With the goal of embodying the bliss, surety, and grace that my pregnant gourd-woman portrays, I move into the last two months of my pregnancy. I am at peace. I know I have done everything I can. If I end up with another cesarean, I will accept it, knowing that I held back nothing.

Laura still wants to "wait and see" before committing to a home delivery. Dr. Vikson, unaware that I am also working with Laura, is preparing me for a cesarean delivery. Though this plan has been clear from the beginning, its conflict disturbs me. Like an obsessed two-year-old, I find myself saying the same thing over and over to both of them: "I know I will probably have a cesarean. All I want is the opportunity to try for a natural delivery. If there are complications, I won't fight the cesarean."

They both nod as if they understand, but their language and the preparations don't change. Hospital policy is hospital policy, and everyone is working from a place of fear. With a history like mine, it is not rational for anyone to expect anything different this time. They cannot understand that I am not the same person I was before.

As the due date nears, the hospital wants me to either turn in the fifteen hundred dollars to keep the operating staff ready or schedule a cesarean. "Do you want me to note in your chart that you want to wait for early labor signs before scheduling?" Dr. Vikson suggests, giving me the language to refuse hospital protocol even without my asking her to.

Does this mean she knows about Laura? What if she doesn't know and finds out later and is angry with me? I need to be able to trust my doctor. How can I trust her, if she can't trust me? So much of this pregnancy has been about uncovering and revealing. I hate being secretive with the person who, when I show up ready to push, will catch my baby. *Will she be disappointed in me?*

Crying, I call to ask Laura for permission to tell Dr. Vikson the truth: that I'm working with a midwife and plan to labor at home. Though I know hospital policy will force her to drop me as I client, I don't want to lie any longer. This way I can be a regular home-birth transfer, if needed.

Laura, listening to me babble about "coming clean," says, with hesitation in her voice, "I've been thinking of trying to push at home. But," she cautions, "we still need to talk more about it."

It doesn't matter how many qualifiers she adds. For the first time I hear her saying that she will give me the chance to birth at home, that she *believes* I might be able to do it. The burden of being the strong one, of proving myself, is lifted from my shoulders. Ridiculously pleased, my tears are of tears of joy.

In the cold and rainy Pacific Northwest winter, worlds away from Hawaii's lush flowers and green forests, the children and I start our annual amaryllis bulb. We water the dirt and check each day for the small sprout that will soon shoot up and burst into flower. I think about the baby and imagine my body opening like a flower to birth her. That's what the books say: "Open like a flower." It sounds cheesy to me, so I don't say it out loud. I only think it. But I buy quite a few of the bulbs to gift, enjoying the idea of family and loved ones around the country growing flowers with me.

Thanksgiving, Solstice, Christmas, Hannukah, and New Year's pass. I, who in spite of the multiple bodies in my bed, sleep as deeply as a teenager the morning after a Red Bull–laced all-nighter, rarely dream (so much as I can remember). But I have a vivid dream about giving birth.

"Were you at home?" Laura asks. "What position were you in? Who was there?"

I consider lying, telling her that it was at home and in my own bed, as if this would convince her that that's where I belong. But the thought of lying to Laura shames me. Surrendering to the truth, I answer honestly: "I don't remember, Laura. Those details were irrelevant. What I remember was the ring of fire—the crowning. There was a giant yoni, and everything came out of it. There were mountains and oceans with fish and dolphins, cities and roads and birds and the sun and moon and stars. The entire world came out."

My throat constricts, trying to stop me from speaking. But even before Laura can "Mmm-hmmm," I force the air through, my voice breaking as I continue. "I think that must be what it's like, because even though a moon doesn't come out of a woman, the ability to see and know and experience what the moon is does." Refusing to hold anything back, I add: "It's not about avoiding a cesarean anymore, Laura. I want to give birth. I want to push my baby from my body. I want it the way I want to breathe. I need to do it."

Crying with me, Laura holds me.

I am in no hurry to deliver this baby. I am painfully aware these are the last days and weeks I will live with the *possibility* of a natural birth. Soon it will be over, herstory. For now, there is the hope, and that in itself is sweet. I cherish it.

Meanwhile, my body is preparing me for birth. Its plan: to make me as uncomfortable as possible so birthing pains become preferable to being pregnant. It begins its attack on my left hip, where it routinely sends sharp pains into my bones. Actually my whole left side seems off. This could be because of my diligent adherence to optimal fetal positioning, which has me sitting straight up, pelvis tipped forward, all the time and sleeping only on my left side in an attempt to coax the baby into the best position to birth from.[18] I refuse to relax my posture; my body will just have to adjust. But I do reduce my daily exercise from three miles of jogging to two miles of slow walking. Even with the decrease, I often need to stop to catch my breath and rub my legs. It takes a full two hours to complete the two miles. I do it anyway.

To prepare the boys for the birth, I bring them to the new sibling class at the hospital, where we take a tour and watch a short film. I want them to know about the hospital, in case I end up here. Avram doesn't speak but watches silently. *Is he afraid? Does he remember Jonah's birth?* Jonah, who still talks to the baby and touches my belly on a daily basis, loves the class. With much determination, he masters the art of diaper changing on a doll that looks and feels like a real baby.

The baby is due on January 22nd, Jonah's birthday. Though I fully expect labor to arrive two weeks late like it did with the other births, we celebrate his birthday a week early, just in case. I give him his own baby doll so he can practice changing diapers and sharing my lap. He is enthralled and takes the "baby" (which is almost as big as he is) everywhere with him.

Mom, Stella, and my girlfriends again offer a blessing way, and again I refuse. They have known the "old" me, the resistant and unfeeling one, for so long that her shadow still stands between us, obscuring who I have become. I don't want it to intrude on any part of my birth.

They gift me small treasures: candles to burn during labor, goddess pictures, cotton caps, receiving blankets, and mochi from my mom. All the big things on our to-do list are done except for putting the birth tub together. Ben promises to do that soon.

"How about acupuncture?" Stella suggests one day as she, mom, and I visit in my kitchen over a cup of tea.

"That's a great idea," Mom says. "You know I went to acupuncture school?"

As it turns out, Stella always wanted to learn acupuncture.

Uh. Oh.

Nervous, I butt in: "You were in acupuncture school over thirty years ago, and you never actually practiced."

Feigning deafness, Mom responds directly to Stella: "The points are easy ones."

"Yes, I know where they are," Stella agrees, having used acupressure on the same points in her midwifery training.

Protesting, I remind them both: "You can't just go out and buy needles; you need to be certified."

It turns out that if you know the right people, you can get needles FedEx-ed to you from out of state without being certified.

A few days later, needles in hand, Mom and Stella coerce me into relaxing by having me sit with my feet in a warm lavender footbath. Then they turn on me.

"You just put it right there and flick it in," Mom says, handing Stella a needle.

"Like that?"

"Ouch," I complain, more playful than hurt.

"Yeah, but faster. Like this."

"I think I got it."

"Agh!" I glare at them.

"Whoops, that's not the point. Try again down a little. It's okay, just a little blood." She says, wiping it away with her thumb.

"This is fun," Stella says.

"Fun for who?" I say. "I'm the pincushion."

Eventually they find all of the points they are looking for and leave me to my "treatment" while they enjoy tea in the kitchen. I hear them softly visiting together, clearly enjoying one another. Half asleep in the other room, I smile to myself. I understand that language now.

13 Merbaby

My body being the size of a whale has not put a stop to the family bed, though it has put a damper on midnight frolicking. Lying on my left side in an attempt to keep the baby in the best position for birth means that one kid gets to be in front of me while the other one is in back. Of course, nobody wants to be in back. Every night Ben and I solve this by each taking one kid in front, which works reasonably well.

January 17th, just before midnight, I wake to find myself sandwiched between two squirming and crying boys, both trying to be in front of me. *Why is Ben not here to take one of them?* I'm not worried; I'm annoyed. He probably fell asleep downstairs. I quiet the children, but my temper does not cool. I'm pregnant and tired and I need help. Wide awake now, I decide that "being heard" is much more important than sleeping, so I heave my two hundred plus pounds of self out of bed and waddle downstairs.

Ben is drinking a beer and watching TV. He looks happy and relaxed and *skinny.* This makes me really mad. In my most pissy voice, I lay into him. "We have a ton to do tomorrow. I need your help in the morning. I could go into labor at any time, and you still haven't set up the birth tub." Without breaking stride, I both realize and say at the same time: "And my water just broke."

My wonderful husband ignores my tone, drops everything, and is completely with me. I look down to verify the warm drip. It's not the clear amniotic fluid I expected. It's blood. Ben helps me back upstairs, where I go straight to the toilet and, shaking, sit down. *There isn't supposed to be blood.* Ben calls Laura.

A bloody, egg-sized mass slips from me. Blood is on my thighs, dripping down my legs and onto the floor. I scream for the phone. Laura promises to come right over.

With kids asleep all over our family bed, Ben helps me to the boys' room, putting me on the bottom bunk. It creaks loudly against my weight. To distract me, he makes a joke about breaking the bed. I manage a small smile in response. Ben lights candles and covers me with enormous blankets. I'm shaking, my teeth are rattling. I can't control it. I'm scared. I remember Dr. Vikson saying that she thinks something is wrong with the placenta. Should I be in the hospital? What is happening?

It seems to take forever for Laura to arrive. She listens to the baby with a fetoscope and looks in the toilet at the bloody mass. Making firm contact with my eyes she says, "It's okay; your baby is fine. Labor sometimes starts with bleeding."

She goes on, explaining the different things the clot could be, but I don't hear her words. I'm watching her. Her movements are quiet, her voice is calm. She isn't scared. I trust her. My body relaxes its shaking. My heart believes her. My baby is okay.

Laura gives me little pH strips to test the fluid flowing from me to confirm whether it's amniotic fluid. *What else could it be—beet juice?* The paper turns black: amniotic fluid. This means, surges or not, the baby will be here soon. I try to feel happy and excited, but I cannot shake this feeling of predictability. Labor can start in so many ways besides the water breaking, but it's starting the same way as the previous two labors, except this time with blood. I'm painfully aware that now, a full five days before the due date, and two weeks before I expected labor, the clock is ticking and this baby had better come quickly.

As there are no surges yet, I'm sent to bed to sleep for as long as I can. After a few hours I awake to a few minor surges. They are not painful, but I can't sleep any more. I need to have this baby ASAP. I resolve to walk myself into labor, but on my way down to the treadmill, I think of my walks along the ocean in Hawaii. I don't want to be in the basement in front of a TV. I want to go out into the world. I want to see the sunrise.

Bundling up, I head out into the soft light that comes just before a winter dawn without stopping to brush my teeth or put in contact lenses. There are lots of people out and walking, which surprises me. I was expecting to be alone. At a steady pace, I aim for the top of the highest close hill.

Hearing an alarm in the distance, I wonder if it's the town emergency system. *Maybe the dam broke.* A little half-hearted laugh escapes my lips. *Strange thought.* Someone with a dog passes me—I imagine it attacking me. *This is crazy. I'm paranoid.*

I turn and head back down the hill. I want to be home. I see a man seated in a car. The car is not moving. *Is he dead?* These are not rational thoughts. I know it, and I know that it's not really a dam or dog or a man sitting in a car that scares me. It's labor. Sternly, I tell myself to get it together and be brave. Picking up the pace, I arrive home tired, with minor surges, and let myself sleep.

Waking much later, with no surges, I clear the calendar for the next few days. This I know: when I labor, I labor for days. I arrange pickups and play dates for the kids, clean the house, and cook a meal. By afternoon I am ready. The only thing missing is surges. This is not good. It still might work out, but it's not good.

Laura gives me herbs. Nothing.

I have an appointment with a real acupuncturist. No surges.

The bleeding continues, but it's minor now, just a few drops. I haven't told friends and family yet. I'm not ready for them to start watching the clock. I put the little ones to sleep right after dinner, hoping the surges will begin the moment they drop off and I'm free to relax. Though I have a couple of minor surges, this is not labor and I know it. I think of the days without labor prior to Avram's delivery, and I pray for it to begin soon.

I check the pH again the next day. This time the result shows no amniotic fluid. I sleep and wake; again no surges and no amniotic fluid. I'm grateful that Laura does not mention the hospital. Even better, as the pH continues to show no amniotic fluid, Laura offers to call it a fluke. She says maybe I just lost bladder control, maybe there was just blood.

"Maybe," I agree. But the pH strip was black. At my doubting look, Laura suggests that mysterious things can happen and that leaks sometimes seal themselves. I'm not sure that hospital policy or Dr. Vikson would agree, but I'm not in their hands. I'm at home. Policy and fear don't have to dictate my thinking. *Laura trusts my body, why don't I?*

I try to be grateful that the bleeding stopped, but my fear won't settle. I haven't even reached my due date yet, much less the two weeks after that, when I had expected labor to begin. Though the surges tease me night and day, they aren't intense; more what a doctor would call Braxton Hicks

And the amaryllis bulb, the one that was supposed to flower along with my body, still has just one quarter of an inch of green sticking out of the bulb, the same quarter of an inch that was there two weeks ago. It's dead. I'm sure of it—almost sure. If I were really sure, I would throw it out. It's just like me. No labor. No baby. No flower.

It's hard to get up. It's hard to lie down. I lose my breath, my feet are swollen, and I'm taking handfuls of pills three times a day. I never want to eat protein again. Beef liver should be outlawed. I'm tired but can't sleep because my hips hurt. I don't want eggs for breakfast, protein powder for snack, and meat for lunch and dinner. I'm especially miserable as I watch Ben and the boys eating pizza. It looks good. It smells good. It's on my "no" list. Instead of joining them, I pace and nibble on cold chicken while talking with my friend Linda on the phone. She is in mid sentence when I'm pulled under by a surge so strong that I can't hold the phone. So I reach out to hand it to Ben.

"Is it for me?" he asks, taking another bite of pizza as he takes the phone from my hand.

"Oouuuuhhh," I answer.

There are two rules to follow in the presence of a laboring woman. The first is: Don't talk, move, think or breathe when she is in the middle of a surge. In all fairness, Ben does not know I'm having a "real" surge this time. But rule two is that you must know everything going on with the woman without being told. Therefore Ben is breaking both rules.

"For me?" he repeats while chewing a mouth full of pizza.

Doubled over from the surge, I am unable to talk. I tilt my head sideways and glare into his eyes, willing him to shut up.

Oblivious, he asks, "Who is it?"

Summoning supreme effort, I make a swatting gesture with my hand.

"Is someone on the phone?"

The surge fades, rendering me able to speak. Grabbing the phone back from Ben, I snarl "contraction" and stomp away.

Linda, having heard the exchange, recognizes the voice of labor. She tells me she is honored that I answered the phone to speak to her right now, that she is thinking of me, sending love, and will light a candle for me. In response I burst out sobbing. Finding myself snarling at my husband is a normal experience, but sobbing at a friend's sweet comments is not. This is how I know I'm now really in labor.

I'm in labor.

I call to tell Laura, who suggests that I try to sleep. "If it's a fluke, it will go away. If not, at least you will get the chance to rest."

Resting slows the surges, but each one is strong enough to jolt me back awake. There is no way I can sleep through these. Half an hour later I call her again. "Please come," I beg.

Every surge brings pain in my hips, making it difficult to relax. It hurts to stand. It hurts to lie down. I try putting a hot water bottle over my hip. Stupid idea. I had forgotten rule number three: no touching or pressure during a surge.

My boys are attentive, unusually quiet, and sweet. Avram brings me a glass of water and a bowl to throw up in. Wide-eyed, he is careful to not wiggle or talk during surges. He is scared. I think of his own and his brother's births and how they were both so difficult for him. Seeing another surge coming, he creeps up and softly holds my hand till the end. My sweet boy. I want him to experience a natural birth. I want to write over his previous birth experiences. Watching his bravery gives me strength and fills me with pride at his love and care for me.

Ben holds a cup of Mom's boiled ginseng concoction to my lips. I turn my head away, refusing it. This is enough. It hurts too much. I don't want it to get more intense. But he won't take it away. "Drink some first," he tells me.

I don't have it in me to refuse it. Drinking this black liquid with its unidentifiable floating bits is easier than explaining or talking. It tastes just like one would expect a root that was boiled for thirty days to taste: nasty. Ben, preparing for days of labor, disappears to get the kids ready for bed, telling Jonah, "Maybe the baby will come tomorrow, on your birthday, but maybe not. Babies take a long time."

I'm relieved when Laura arrives. She watches quietly. Taking a fetoscope out of her bag, she listens to the baby's heartbeat between surges. Following our agreement, she does not check to see how dilated I am—my labors last long and I don't want to feel pressure to perform. At least that's what I wanted when we agreed to not do regular checks. But now that I'm in labor, I would really like to know how soon it will be over. Then again, I might not like her answer, and "uhhhhhh" I would have to lie down and hold still for a check, and "uuuuhhhhhhh. . . ."

Ben pops his head in and cheerily reminds me: "Breathe through your mouth."

"Ooohhhhhh." If I wasn't overcome with a contraction, I would punch him.

Laura, seeing me glare at the empty door where Ben's head had been, announces that it's time fill the tub. This serves as confirmation that labor is progressing quickly, as water relieves labor but if used too early will slow progress.

Ben, who had never gotten around to putting the tub together, looks for the pieces. Laura goes into the living room to sort through her supplies. I'm alone. This is not okay. They are talking and moving around the house and I'm alone and I'm in labor and it hurts and they are busy screwing around. "Ooooohhhh" (louder this time to announce my displeasure). Laura returns to explain that tub pieces are missing. My hips are killing me. The surges are really intense, and they can't find the fucking tub pieces. *Incompetent fools.* I yell: "Check in the red car underneath all the rest of that shit."

Somehow they think this is funny. Laughing, they disappear together.

Between surges, Avram helps Ben put the tub together. During surges, everyone must hold perfectly still and follow rule number one. They get nowhere fast with the tub, so Laura sends me to the other room, where I squat over a pad. I don't like it. I don't want to be alone. Sensing this, she comes to sit with me. She does not say or do anything, but her presence is a gift. By her not talking or comforting or directing, there is room for me to fully experience. She bears witness and in doing so honors me.

As soon as the tub is half full, I strip. Inhibitions be damned. There isn't enough water and it's not really warm, but it lifts the weight from my muscles, supporting me, soothing and softening my body. The pain in my hips dissipates. I experience immediate relief. The water is divine. I want only to float here in peace.

Except that I have to poop. When the surge ends, I quickly jump out to take care of business. Getting back to the tub before the next surge hits is imperative. Relieved that this is done. I sink into the water and again will my body to soften.

Except that I need to poop. *Didn't this just happen?*

I repeat the process. Again and again and again. This is ridiculous. Nobody told me about this. It wasn't in the videos. How am I supposed to concentrate and relax and breathe and poop all at once? My whole life up until now I've pooped just once a day and then been done. I expected that to continue. Nope. Each surge brings more poop. The ultimate colonic. *God please don't make me get out of the water.* Either she doesn't hear me or she doesn't care because the poop keeps coming. You would think I would run out of poop but I don't. It's endless poop.

My ego, having (literally) had enough of this shit, quits. It gets up and walks right out the door. What is left of me poops in the tub. Looking down, I say, "ewwww." I say it as if it wasn't me who just shat in the tub. I say it as if I just happened to come across poop in my bath one day. "Ewwww" or not, I'm never getting out of the tub ever again. If this tub were full of nothing but shit mud, I would still stay right here.

Another surge begins. My mind, unable to follow my ego out the door, recedes deep into my body, releasing the outside world. As the surge ends, I see, outside of my body, a light is shining. My eyes follow the beam back to a flashlight held by my beautiful midwife. She is leaning over the birth tub, fishnet in hand. She is fishing out my poop.

"That is a fishnet."

"Yes," Laura agrees.

I open my mouth to laugh but another surge stops me, and I fade, once more, into my own body. The rest of the world is far away. I open my mouth, deep guttural "uuuuuuhhhhhhhhh" sounds come out, and the surge fades. *Where is Ben?*

Between surges, I flail around the tub, grabbing its soft edges and yelling at Laura. "This is not fun."

There is a ping. A poof of soft pink comes from inside me. Little bits of white vernix float around the water. I look for Laura's eyes. My voice breaking, I announce, "My water broke."

"It's okay," she reassures.

She is wrong. It's not okay. It means that this is going to get harder. I'm really not in the mood for this now. In fact, I would like to just postpone this whole thing and try again another day. I open my mouth to tell her this, but before the words form, another surge brings me down. I'm on all fours in the tub.

Ben returns, finally. He takes one quick look at me and, summing up the situation in a manly way, tells me to relax and says to Laura that I'm not handling the "contractions" well. I open my mouth to yell "Asshole," but before I get to the double "s" a surge brings me back down so all that comes out is "aaaaaaaaaa," which sounds just like what I've been saying. Laura, being a midwife, knows what I meant to say and gets him to shut up and sit quietly at the edge of the tub. I lunge toward him, displacing large amounts of water onto the carpet, and press my head into his hands, needing connection. During surges nothing exists but the pain. I scream loudly (later described as rhino-like). I'm lost in it. It hurts.

In the brief moments of stillness between the waves, my left brain returns to protest. *This is too hard. I cannot do this. I want it over.* If a stranger walked in and offered me a cesarean right now, I would accept without hesitation. *I need drugs.* Knowing that midwives don't have drugs, I muster every bit of remaining articulation to say "Tylenol."

Veege, the assistant midwife (where did she come from?), brings ice. If I knew the words to use, I would explain that ice is not an adequate substitute for drugs, but I have forgotten what those words would be and there are not enough moments between surges to get the ice into my mouth and also find words. I use both hands, shoveling in as much ice as possible. Needing to swallow before the next surge begins, I chew and gulp all at once, ice chips raining from my mouth, scattering on the floor while I desperately push more in before the next surge begins.

"Mom," I beg.

The cry is primal. An entire lifetime is forgotten, leaving only this same cry that I made when I was first separated from my own mother's body: "mother"—womb, breath, warmth, heartbeat, security. A lifetime of choosing men over women, of believing that I'm capable and strong without a mother, crumbles into nothingness, washed away in an ocean of surges. Ben leaves me to call her to come.

The waves are beyond managing. When I feel one start, I try to breathe, try to open up, but each time I lose it. Feeling my whole body convulse, I need to articulate the problem to Laura, need help fixing it, but all that comes out is "down. . . ." Trying again, "down. . . ." but another surge brings me beyond thought. The dance has changed. I am pushing.

There is an enormous pressure in my ass. The Hypnobirthing CD plays in the background. I haven't heard it since I was in labor with Jonah. It has the gall to tell me: "Your baby moves gently into the vaginal opening. Imagine that opening to be like a rose bud. See the petals of the rose slowly and easily unfolding and opening to allow the baby to slip out."

There is nothing flowerlike about this. It's not soft or gentle or sweet smelling. This is a stretching torture machine complete with a wrecking ball ramming into my bones, forcing apart sockets that have been firmly in place for my entire existence. It's rearranging my innards with complete disregard. My pelvis is breaking open. I am an obstacle. My body is irrelevant. I could not have imagined this violence, this betrayal from nature. Birth is happening through me, in spite of me, and with complete disregard for my being.

I see Death in the corner of the room, grinning gleefully. She is waiting to see what will become of what was once my body and is now nothing more than Creation's obstacle. There is no warm light, no tunnel, no loved ones waiting to greet me. There are blood and guts and shit and pain and the destruction of a woman's body. My body. Deep inside there is stinging. This is my skin ripping open with each downward movement.

Consonants leave me. Vowels scream from my body: *oooooooeeeeeeeeeee!*
I cannot do it. I am not enough. I surrender.

Only then does the Divine come, taking my body as her own. I am no longer alone. There is no fear. I'm ready to birth my daughter. I know what I am doing and my moment is now. Ben is behind me in the water, crying quietly on my shoulder. Avram, Jonah, and my mother, with tears in her eyes, stand by the side of the tub and watch quietly. Unseen but equally present, our ancestors bears witness.

Where before there was pain, now there is only exquisite pleasure. Reaching inside of the body that used to confine me, I feel my baby's head. It is soft and wrinkly and covered with thick hair. Orgasmic Amazon Queen carries the head out of my body, half born, still me but now more. I experience completeness. I find religion. Infinity is tangible. Generations of children, their dreams, passions, defeats, and glories—they all pass through me, converging here, between my thighs: a beautiful, shining ball covered in thick black hair.

Too quickly—I would have stayed in this moment forever if it had been allowed—the next surge comes, shooting her, like a rocket, out in a cloud of pink fluid. In front of me, bobbing face down in the water is a blue and purple merbaby.

There is no interference. No sound. First contact is mine by right. I reach for my baby and, instinctively, do what every uninterrupted mother since the beginning of time has done. I cradle her to my left side, to my heart, to where the first sound she hears is the steady and familiar beat of home. She is slippery like a dolphin and oh so soft. The bright cord, still pulsing food and oxygen, entwines us.

My baby, announcing life, screams loudly. My ripped vagina and my family, are still in another world. I know only what I must do, what I have needed to do from the moment my first baby was stolen from me.

"I'm here. It's okay. I've got you. I'm here. It's okay. I've got you. I'm here. It's okay. I've got you. . . ." This is all I have to offer, and it is everything that matters.

The moment her eyes find mine, she quiets, recognizing me though we have never seen each other. We are even more connected than when we were still one body.

In time I announce what my heart has known all along. "It's a girl." Our audience erupts with a cheer, other voices filling the air, welcoming my daughter. Laughter. Crying. Celebration.

She was born at 11:57 pm on January 21st, just four hours after I first called Laura, and three minutes before Jonah's birthday. Rhione, the second midwife, only now arrives; Laura hadn't had the chance to finish setting up. There are details to sort out, missing blankets, caps, and tools to find. They search gently and quietly, their headlamps set on low. But I haven't come back to the present yet. The past and future are equally tangible. I bark, "Quiet! Turn off the lights!" I'm not talking to the midwives. I'm talking to the doctors and nurses and anesthesiologists. To the people who, with gloved hands, pulled my babies from my body into cold air and bright lights. The people who were so busy doing their medical stuff that they did not recognize that my babies were screaming for me. Time folds as I, witnessed by my sons, claim my mother's rights. Laura, Rhione, and Veege, respectful of my authority, bustle around in the dark looking for their tools.

As I start to return to the confines of my body, it begins shaking. I deliver the placenta. Avram cuts the cord while Jonah watches silently. It is perfectly natural that they are here, that they were part of their sister coming into the world. Ready to leave the tub, I choose when to hand my baby over for the first time to the waiting arms of her family. The shaking becomes uncontrollable now. Veege puts warm blankets around me. As briefly as possible, Laura and Rhione do a quick check on the baby. Then the midwives and my mother exit to the kitchen to give our family time alone.

She is beautiful. The boys do not have anything to say. They do not play or argue or whine. All of us want only to smell and touch and look at this baby. A few short hours ago, there were only four in our family. Now and forever more we are five.

Laura returns with the placenta in a large kitchen bowl. "This was the baby's home," she tells the two very intrigued boys. "This is the 'tree of life.' See how the cord is like a trunk and the arteries stretch out like branches?"

"There is something unusual about your placenta, Roanna," she says, spreading it out with gloved hands so I can see. "It is not a single circle but has this smaller, second lobe."

It looks like a second placenta but without a "tree of life." Dr. Vikson was right; there was something "wrong" with my placenta. This second lobe was likely the cause of the bleeding in early pregnancy as well as the reason why the first membrane tore days before. But she was also wrong. My placenta took good care of my baby, and I gave birth naturally and safely.

Coming back to my body, I'm hungry. I want pancakes. After the cesareans, I never wanted to eat. Nothing sounded, smelled, or tasted good. Now here I am, babe in arms, eating. Strange to think that just five hours ago I was trying to prepare myself for days of labor.

Seeing the boys rub their eyes, Mom takes them into the other room to put them to sleep on the bunk beds. They want to sleep with us and resist being alone in their room until Mom lies with them, softly patting their backs and singing "Baby Owlet" until they fall asleep.

Meanwhile, Laura checks for tearing. Lying still, legs spread like a porn star, my body hurts. I hadn't anticipated this part. There are no pain killers. It feels like sharp, metallic prickling reaching inside of me, deep past the vaginal opening. Laura asks: "Would you like stitches?

"They are optional?" I ask.

"You'll be fine as long as you don't open your legs for a while."

"I will never, ever open my legs again," I reply, quite seriously.

"Mmm-hmmm," Laura smiles.

My overwhelming feeling is love for my new daughter. *I gave birth.*

The midwives and my mother ask if there is anything more I want before they leave. I look around. The room is clean and quiet. A full jug of water lies within reach. Ben is with me; our daughter is naked on a lambskin between us, but something is missing: my boys. At my request they are carried in and, still fast asleep, placed next to us in bed. We are now five.

14 Amaryllis and Dalia

Everybody says vaginal recoveries are easier than cesareans. Today, the day after birthing my daughter, I don't believe them. I fondly recall the drugs, the mind-numbing, fuzzying drugs, separating me from my body, that they gave me after the cesareans.

I had thought that natural birth, being natural, would be easy, right? Wrong. Tearing, I had tearing all wrong. I thought tears were like stretch marks or surface scratches or maybe a little split in my labia. This is not what tearing is. Tearing is when your body stretches until your skin rips open. Completely open, flesh-exposed open. It starts up high in the vaginal canal and goes all the way down to the opening, which is tender and swollen like a giant beach ball.

Needing to pee, out of habit I sit on the toilet, but pop up immediately as the pressure opens the cuts. Exposed to air, they sting painfully. So I stand to pee. Think of lemon juice on a cut. Now imagine multiple cuts deep inside you. That's what it feels like to pee. At this moment, I would pay any price for a catheter.

I have exactly what I wished for and dreamed of, the greatest and most fought-for accomplishment of my life. But I find myself traumatized by it. I had no idea it would be so violent. When I had the cesareans, I was a victim. *They* did it to me. I lived in an "if only" dream for four years. I was sure that if they hadn't cut me open, I would have opened like a flower. I would have stayed calm and controlled through the whole thing. I would have been perfect.

The reality of birth was nothing like I had imagined. I was not a strong warrior; I did not gently breathe my baby into the world. It was not pretty. It was not like the videos. I screamed. I lunged. I whined. I glared and swore. There was nothing ladylike or dignified or graceful about me.

I now see through the pretty bubble we put around ourselves. If it hurts, we take drugs. If we don't want to know about it, we close the paper or change the channel. We know death is inevitable, so we tell stories of tunnels and light and loved ones and angels. We plump up our dead with chemicals to keep them firm and smelling fresh. We paint their faces with pretty makeup. This is not what death looks like. Death looks like shit and blood and guts. We are utterly and completely unimportant in the face of nature. We have no vote. This is not a democracy. In my wildest imaginings, I would never have believed that the goddess would betray me, would violate her own daughter this way.

It must be some sort of cosmic joke that by achieving my greatest dream, by discovering the magnificence of birth, I'm confronted by my own irrelevance. Humbled, I know I have accomplished nothing. What happened, happened through me, in spite of me, and with complete disregard for my existence.

The one thing more important than all else is my daughter. She has the most beautiful eyes I have ever seen. They are exotic, I've never experienced any quite like them, yet I know them as intimately as if they were my own. Tracing her brow with my fingertip, I am content to while away the hours looking into their depths. I luxuriate in staying in bed all day and doing just that. Family and Laura come to visit and check on us, to marvel with me at my daughter's perfection, to measure and weigh her, to touch her toes and watch her fierce nursing.

Avram's placenta was disposed of as "hazardous waste." Jonah's I brought home, froze (planning to plant it under a tree), and promptly forgot. But this one—this one Ben makes soup with. French onion. It is delicious. Really. Before you overreact, consider that the nutritional content of the placenta, full of iron, makes it a specially designed food for a woman who has just gone through birth. Many mammals eat their placentas. Traditional Chinese medicine uses it for a variety of ailments. It's also the only meat that can be eaten without taking a life.

I admit, at first I was a little apprehensive, but eating it feels good. I feel powerful. Next time I'm going to eat it raw. *"Next time"—where did that come from? Just yesterday I promised to never open my legs again.*

French Onion and Placenta Soup
Makes about five 8 oz servings

½ cup butter
4 onions, peeled, and thin sliced
3 garlic cloves, minced
3 bay leaves
2 fresh thyme sprigs
1/4 fresh placenta, or 35 placenta pills
    if you've had yours encapsulated
1 cup red wine
3 TBL all-purpose flour
4 cups water, beef, placenta, or chicken broth
Salt and pepper to taste
Sourdough bread, cubed
8 oz Gruyere or Swiss cheese, grated

Sauté, stirring regularly, the butter, onions, garlic, baby leaves, thyme, a pinch of salt and few grinds of pepper, until the onions are translucent. Meanwhile, remove the cord, membranes, and any clots from the placenta. Rinse it under cold water. Quarter it, set three quarters aside for another use, and add the remaining quarter to the sauté. Remove placenta when it is cooked through. Slice thin and set aside.

Continue cooking the onions, stirring regularly, until they become brown. Add wine and simmer until the liquid evaporates and the onions lose their form. Add flour. Mix well. With a low flame, cook, stirring regularly, for 5 minutes. Add water, beef, placenta or chicken stock, and sliced placenta. Simmer for 10 minutes. Season with salt and pepper to taste.

To serve: preheat broiler. In oven-friendly serving bowls or pot, cover the hot soup with cubed sourdough bread and the bread with grated cheese. Broil until the cheese melts and begins to brown. Serve immediately.

On the fourth day after the birth, Mom, in front of Laura, mentions that I should lay low for the first month. Until she said this I had no desire to get out of bed, but nothing makes a daughter want to move more than a mother telling her she ought to rest. I look at Laura and smirk, the kind of smirk that says, "Yeah, right, like that's going to happen."

"Actually, she needs to stay home for forty days," Laura replies without missing a beat.

My jaw drops. I look to make sure she is joking. She is not. She and my mother both start talking at once, building off of one another, each telling me how important it is for me to stay home. How I can't lift anything but the baby. How I can't stand for long or get up except to go to the bathroom. Mom, confident that Laura will enforce this and knowing I will put up less resistance without her being present, leaves the room.

I protest, "How did this detail not come up before?"

"It took forty weeks for your body to grow a baby," Laura says. "Give it at least forty days before you leave the house. I know other people leave right away, but that doesn't mean it's right. You need to stay home and let your body recover. This is ancient wisdom that used to be taken for granted. Not doing this is one of the reasons why so many women end up with hysterectomies."

The authority in her voice is not debatable. This is not the Laura who asked me about my intuition and dreams, the one whose questions brought me deeper into myself to find my own answers, the one who trusted me to know what I need. I have never seen her so adamant about anything. She has never said "no" to me before. On her way out, she adds "no stairs" to the order, rendering my office, computer, and work a non-option.

"What am I supposed to do?" I ask.

"Write your birth story," she answers, smiling.

Before this, I hadn't thought to even leave my room. But I don't like to be told what to do, so the moment they leave I get up and walk around the house. My small home feels huge. There is clutter in the living room and dishes in the kitchen sink. The floor needs to be swept. I am surrounded by things to pick up, tasks to do. This is not nearly as fun as I had imagined. Feeling slightly overwhelmed, I see the kitchen counter, where, in full bloom, a bright red flower beckons me. It is the thought-dead amaryllis.

Standing alone in my kitchen, I feel much like the maiden named Amaryllis must have felt when, according to Greek mythology, she used blood from her own heart to create a red bloom for her true love. Touching the velvet petals, I feel a wet tear cool on my cheek. I take the flower back to my room without pausing. Someone else can clean.

My daughter also is not ready to venture out. I will know when she is because her eyes, her most beautiful eyes, will look out into the world; her vision for the first time will reach beyond my face.

Mom and Laura are right. Physically, my body is still open; the bones of my hips and pelvis are loose, like pieces of a worn jigsaw puzzle. Torn, raw, and shedding blood, my body wants rest. My emotions, larger than can be contained, tangle together: fear and power, tears and laughter, joy and betrayal. Like a crazy person, I do not sort them but experience them all at once.

When our other newborns arrived, Ben and I, with Mom's help, did all our own cooking. This time, feeling like a deserving queen, I allow a friend to organize meals for us. Friends cook and deliver meals every night for our family of five. Between the meals and my mom's daily help, I quickly learn to enjoy being pampered. Though

I *could* work or shop or cook or take the boys to school, why would I want to? My body, my amazing, wonderful, strong, powerful body, assisted in creating and nourishing another person and then pushed her through my very self and out into the world. I think I'll sit here with my feet propped up for a bit.

One week later: I want to do it again. I want to feel a baby's head between my thighs. I want to experience again one becoming two. My body open, my bones loose. I want to push another baby out. I want to relive it again and again and. . . .

Two weeks later: Up till now, I have only showered or sponge-bathed, but Laura has said I can take my first bath. I wait until my daughter falls asleep, making sure Ben will stay with her.

Submerging my body into the water unexpectedly triggers memories of the birth. They flash so quickly, hundreds of things that I hadn't realized that I had forgotten, important ones, things I had thought would be mine to keep forever. Desperately, my mind tries to capture them, to feel again what it was to be one with the Divine. But the more my left brain tries to close in, the faster She slips away.

Deep inside, I feel the screams of birth echoing off the sides of my scull. Softer and softer they fade, becoming a faint whisper, then disappearing completely.

I open my mouth. "Please," I whisper-scream-beg-cry, "please come back."

She does not.

I am, once again, mortal.

Leaving my tears in the now-cold water, I glance at my reflection in the mirror. Something begs my attention. It's the same reflection, the same me that has always been there. Then I see them: my eyes. I have my daughter's eyes. But I had never known mine were beautiful. Tears in my beautiful eyes, I smile at them.

We name our daughter Dalia. My mother blesses her name with the following poem:

Dalia Rosewood
Speaking on behalf of your grandmothers—
Welcome to this blessed body,
This loving family and community and
To your home
Nestled near Bear Creek
In the Rogue Valley of the Siskiyous
Floating on Turtle Island
We welcome you, Dalia Rosewood

Dalia means "to draw water" in Hebrew
And "ocean" in Mongolian.
It's really not so curious
That a giant, hollow-stemmed dahlia
Named "water cane" by the Aztecs
Was used for hauling water.
Also, the flowers root yields inulin,
A natural medicine healing many.
Is it any wonder that dahlia blossoms
So delight our eyes
And hearts with the tides of love.

And now,
Born under the sign of the water-bearer,
You are Dalia Rosewood.
We thank you for joining us.
We celebrate who you are.
We vow to see you clearly and to
Support you in realizing
Your ultimate freedom.

May you be blessed with a long and fortunate life
May you continue to benefit your family
And all beings

Welcome, Dalia Rosewood,
To this brothy, briny soup.

Grandma

These days with Dalia take on a delightful rhythm. We eat breakfast in bed, cuddle with the boys for a while, then take a nap while Ben gets the boys to school. When I wake again, we venture out into the living room to snuggle near the fire, eat lunch, and look into each other's eyes. Sometimes I lay Dalia down next to me on a large red pillow for a bit while I work on a doll I'm sewing for her or strive to capture the experience of giving birth in writing. Nap time, then back to bed to snuggle and read a book until I fall asleep, followed by dinner and bedtime, then through the night half-waking every couple of hours to nurse, touch, and smell Dalia. I don't want to read about current events. Nothing matters but what is happening inside my own home: my daughter's awakening to the enormous world outside my womb. I want nothing more than to hold her and to honor and pamper my body and the wild ride it brought us through.

Avram, being four, has better things to do than play with Dalia, though he does admit that she is cute. Jonah, however, is in love. He touches her gently, holds her often, and assists with diaper changing. At two, he is still a baby himself, but when he holds her, his eyes light up and his grin stretches farther than his face. He calls her "my baby" and if she fusses at all, insists that she be "nummied" immediately. He never once shows jealousy.

One month after the birth: People in the outer world are asking about me, wondering why I don't make it to the parent-teacher meeting. They "feel bad" that I'm not "able" to go out. Silly fools. I'm the queen this month, I'm taking a vacation at home.

I move around the house more now. Though I'm looking forward to doing some walking, exercise, and making my own meals, I don't want to rush this. Being cared for and loved by family, friends, and my wonderful husband is a treat.

During the postpartum exam, completely uninhibited, I lay spread-eagled on the bed, Dalia curled beside me, while Laura makes sure everything is as it should be. "Nice pink tissues. You will have a small scar where you tore." Putting her fingers inside of me, Laura says, "Kegel."

I do.

Her expression does not change

"Did you feel it?" I ask.

"Well" (not wanting to tell me that my vaginal muscles are gone), "it feels like you just pushed a baby out."

I scowl at her and close my legs.

Laura laughs. "With lots of practice your muscles will return."

On the thirty-eighth day, I have only two more days at home, and I'm crying like a baby. What a silly thing to say. My Dalia doesn't cry. Occasionally she mews like a kitten. She screamed when she was born, but she hasn't cried yet. She is safe and secure in our small world. There has been no overstimulation, no car trips or strangers. What is there for her to cry about? This has been the best month of my life. I don't want it to end.

Having postponed Laura's final visit a couple of times, I have run out of reasons to avoid it. Laura is moving on to other clients. She will share the intimacy of birth with other women, welcome and celebrate other babies. As foolish as it seems, I am jealous. She who mentored and supported me through my most intimate and difficult journey, is leaving me.

Not knowing how to articulate my love for her, I simply thank her and fight the tears that well up in my eyes. Being Laura, she fills the space for both of us, crying and gifting me with me her own appreciation and joy. "I am proud of you, Roanna. You were courageous and strong, and you pushed your baby out. I will remember this. I will remember you. Thank you for sharing your journey with me,"★

★ Watch Laura and Roanna's intimate conversation about birth at visit www. cutstapledandmended.com/bonus.

As time passes, I meet many other moms with Laura Babies (said with the same tone in which some extol a Louie Vuitton). She has quite a following. Just a glimpse of her shopping at Ashland's co-op, picking her kids up from school, or visiting with a mom about to burst brings a smile to my face. When the queues to greet her are short, I wait my turn to look into her eyes and receive a strong hug and moment or two of her undivided attention. Though this is the extent of our relationship now, though my life is full of other deep and cherished friendships, Laura will forever be one of my most favorite people.

15 Bunk Beds

I never intended to embark on a journey of personal transformation; all I wanted was to give birth with my own body. Reading my story now, five years after Dalia was born, I see that I did so much more.

It's hard to acknowledge the person I used to be. I don't like her very much. I never really did. But I understand her. She desperately believed that she was "as good as a man." Therein lay the problem. Men were her baseline. But as wonderful as men are: women are fantastic. Our bodies grow, nurture, and open to bring whole new people into the world. It is our birthright to partner in the creation of life. There is nothing more powerful than this.

I understand why we fear birth and seek to make it a sterile and planned event. But doing so denies us our greatest opportunity: partnership with the divine. It's not possible to numb ourselves to fear, pain, and death without also numbing ourselves to courage, pleasure, and life.

My tough armor has been replaced. I feel not just comfortable but womanly and sexy in my own skin. My old uniform of jeans, a T-shirt, and sneakers has long since been replaced with a closet brimming with finery. Not fancy, prove-things-to-the-world finery. I don't dress to impress. I dress because I love myself and take pleasure in adorning my body with all manner of luscious clothing: silks and velvets, jewels, lace, scarves, and dangling earrings, and a touch of lip color. A nice pair of knee-high heeled boots with a dress is my favorite: the best of both worlds, feminine and strong, just like me.

But my favorite part of being a woman is having girlfriends. I have discovered that women make seriously wonderful friends, and I have the best ones in the world. We laugh, cry, and celebrate life together and bear witness to one another, sharing our stories and understanding each other in a way men really can't.

My relationship with Dalia is girlish and sweet. It's so different than my connection with the boys. Truth be told, for no logical reason, she can also make me madder than the other two combined. Dalia loves me with the same attention, focus, and entwinement that I have been loved with by only one other person: my mother.

Dalia knows where she came from. When she wants to get as close to me as possible, she lifts my shirt and pushes her hands and head into my belly, pressing on it, listening to the sounds it makes, kissing it, caressing it. "I love your belly," she says, making me laugh with pleasure that my flabby and stretch-marked skin provides such joy. We refer to the others in the family collectively as "the boys." Though we love them dearly, it's nice to have someone to sympathize with when they do boy things like tying up the dolls or farting with relish.

Dalia lives life with the same power she came into the world with. Though the youngest, she is the boss, jumping into the boys' wrestling matches full force, playing Spiderwoman in superhero adventure fantasies, and generally keeping things in line without giving up the fierce femininity she was conceived with. The other day, from out of the pink, she announced, "I am not a girl, I am a *woman*."

Jonah is a pretty confident and self-sufficient little guy. His one soft spot is for Dalia. He loves her unconditionally and will do anything she asks, climbing tall trees, more often naked than not, gathering the choicest plums for her, carrying her around, and helping her with her chores. They are inseparable, always holding hands and snuggling together. Though Jonah is an easy-going kid, he's devastated when Dalia rejects him, which she must sometimes do in order to get some breathing space. "Dalia, am I your best friend?" is his favorite question.

This lovey-dovey stuff makes Avram roll his eyes. He thinks Jonah and Dalia are fun to play with, but his heart belongs to Dad. Ben gets the nicest gifts and the first hugs. If Avram is sick at school, it is Ben's cell phone he calls.

This does not bother me. Avram's love for me is deep and real. I never find it lacking. Avram and I share the common experience of being supported by Ben. Those blue eyes that were my lifeline during the pain and confusion of Avram's labor and the horror of his delivery belong to the same man who comforted Avram when he screamed his first request to the world, the first person he saw, the first person who held him. Rather than resenting his adoration of his papa, I enjoy the companionship of uniting with him in loving Ben.

My dreams of children and family have come true. I have exactly what I wanted in life. Along the way, I found something even more important, something I didn't know I was missing: myself.

Yet I know that my story is not so special. Many women have stories more significant than mine: Regina, whose beautiful baby girl died in her arms shortly after birth, did not shrivel up and retreat; instead, her grace inspired and opened the hearts of a community. Dyann, following her father's instructions, gave her newborn son up for adoption without a glimpse of him, and waited thirty years to find him—while Jo-Ann, unable to conceive a second time, raised this same baby with attention and love equal to what she gave her biological son. Debbie gave birth twice in one day, the first time vaginally, the second by cesarean. My cousin Adina gave birth to her daughter in her own home, attended only by untrained family. Julie carried a surrogate baby in her womb, a gift for her friends who wanted to be parents but, being men, could not do so without a woman. Rachel, Olivia, and their two toddler daughters, *munu* (whites) from the East Coast of America, live in an Internally Displaced Persons camp in Northern Uganda. They devote their days to training and also learning from illiterate but experienced birth attendants so the Acholi people, recovering from twenty years of a brutal war, can birth safely even without running water, electricity, or any of the other luxuries that most of us take for granted.★ Their stories are the remarkable ones. All I did was give birth.

Even now, five years after Dalia was born, I still hunger for birth, the fullness of crowning, the burning ring of fire. I don't think that will ever change. But as much as I want to do it again and again, Dalia will be my last baby. The reality is that there is no more room in the bed. Upstairs, fast asleep in the same king-sized bed Dalia was conceived in are Ben, Avram (now ten years old), Jonah (seven) and Dalia (five). Curled in his favorite spot, next to Dalia, is a much older and frail Sky Kitty, who despite having kidney disease still enjoys a good romp.

When I go to bed, I will rearrange their long limbs to make room for myself and marvel that these kids used to be in my belly. I will put my hand on the top of Dalia's head and remember how it felt crashing through my body. Avram will move closer to Ben, and Jonah will sleep through it all.

I may wake up Ben and bring him to the bunk beds. Though the boys picked out the sheets (Spiderman on top for Avram and Little Mermaid on the bottom for Jonah), they never sleep there. Bunk beds might not sound exciting, but they are conducive to interesting positions, allow for great leverage, and are a serious step up from the carpet. We have had some pretty good times on them, though Orgasmic Amazon Queen Sex has only happened that once. Maybe I don't need to channel otherworld feminine energy anymore. Maybe I am complete with my own now.

★ To read about Roanna's time volunteering at this birth center visit www. cutstapledandmended.com/bonus.

Notes

Chapter One

1. Paul Pitchford, *Healing with Whole Foods*, North Atlantic Books (2003).
2. Rebecca Wood, *The New Whole Foods Encyclopedia*, Penguin.

Chapter Three

1. FDA, Office of Science and Technology–Annual Report–Fiscal Year 1995, Ultrasound http://www.fda.gov/cdrh/ost/reports/fy95/ultrasound.html

Chapter Five

1. Michel Odent, *The Scientification of Love*. London: Free Association Books, 2001.

Chapter Six

1. Luz Gibbons and others, "The Global Numbers and Costs of Additionally Needed and Unnecessary Caesarean Sections Performed per Year: Overuse as a Barrier to Universal Coverage." Background Paper, 30, World Health Report (2010) (http://www.who.int/healthsystems/topics/financing/healthreport/30C-sectioncosts.pdf)
2. Marsden Wagner, MD, MS , "Adverse Events Following Misoprostol Induction of Labor," *Midwifery Today* Issue 71 (Autumn 2004) (www.midwiferytoday.com/articles/cytotecwagner71.asp)
3. Henci Goer and Nicette Jukelevics, "Position Paper: The Risks of Cesarean Section for Mother and Baby," *Lamaze International* (2010) (www.lamazeinternational.org/p/cm/ld/fid=126).
4. Nathanael Johnson, "For-profit Hospitals Performing More C-sections," California Watch (September 11, 2010) (californiawatch.org/health-and-welfare/profit-hospitals-performing-more-c-sections-4069).
5. "Surprising Facts About Giving Birth in the United States," BabyCenter.com. August 2011. (www.babycenter.com/0_surprising-facts-about-birth-in-the-united-states_1372273.bc), and Joyce Martin, M.P.H and others, "Births: Final Data for 2007," *National Vital Statistics Reports* 58: 24

(Hyattsville, MD: U.S. Department of Health & Human Services) (http://www.cdc.gov/nchs/data/nvsr/nvsr58/nvsr58_24.pdf).

6. Jennifer Block, "Too Many Women Dying in the U.S. While Having Babies" *Time* (March 13, 2010).

Chapter Seven

1. U.S. Department of Health and Human Services, "Vaginal Birth After Cesarean: New Insights," Evidence Report. Technology Assessment #191. (www.ahrq.gov/downloads/pub/evidence/pdf/vbacup.pdf).

2. Amnesty International, "Deadly Delivery: The Maternal Health Care Crisis in the USA" Amnesty International. London 2010 (www.amnestyusa.org/sites/default/files/pdfs/deadlydelivery.pdf).

3. World Health Organization, "Trends in Maternal Mortality: 1990 to 2008" (Switzerland: World Health Organization, UNICEF, and The World Bank, 2010) (www.who.int/reproductivehealth/publications/monitoring/9789241500265/en/index.html).

4. Rita Henley Jensen, "Why is maternal mortality so high in the U.S.?" at upi.com (July 27, 2012) (www.upi.com/Health_News/2012/07/27/Why-is-maternal-mortality-so-high-in-the-US/WEN-7181343403729/).

5. M. B. Landon and others, "Maternal and Perinatal Outcomes Associated with a Trial of Labor after Prior Cesarean Delivery," *The New England Journal of Medicine* 351 (2004), 2581–2589.

6. Marsden Wagner, MD, MS, *Born in the USA: How a Broken Maternity System Must be Fixed to Put Women and Children First.* (Berkley: University of California Press, May 2008).

Chapter Nine

1. Osman and Mirosola, LLP, "Cytotec," (www.oshmanlaw.com/pharmaceutical_litigation/cytotec.html) and Marsden Wagner, MD, MS, "Cytotec Induction and Off-Label Use" *Midwifery Today* Issue 67 (Fall 2003) (www.midwiferytoday.com/articles/cytotec.asp).

2. Nathanael Johnson, "For-profit Hospitals Performing More C-sections," California Watch (September 11, 2010) (californiawatch.org/health-and-welfare/profit-hospitals-performing-more-c-sections-4069).

Acknowledgements

Now that it's done, I see how foolish it was to attempt to fit my life and you, my dear loved ones, into little black letters on paper. I ask for your forgiveness and thank you for sharing this journey with me.

Avram, Jonah and Dalia, being your mother is my greatest honor. Every single day I am awed by the simple pleasure of sharing this life with you. Growing you in my womb and your births, all three of them, were magical and transformative for me. I am filled with joy at the incredible people you are.

Mom and Dad, thank you for giving me life, for raising me with love, teaching me that my health is my own response-ability, and encouraging and inspiring me to bushwhack my own path through life.

I am grateful to my siblings. Asa steps forward with determination against even the most trying challenges. Eliza is my artistic entrepreneurial go-to person and a driving force behind this book. Sarah inspires me to take her lead and just be myself without worrying what anyone else thinks. And Kelly brings joy and fun to even the darkest times.

I believe that Verna and Mel Wood and Belle and Leon Atkind are the absolute best grandparents in the world. While it would fill two pages to mention all of my cousins, aunts, uncles, and one single nephew, (will somebody rectify this please ;-) you all fill my heart. Emma, Diana, and Marc: family.

My beloved, you protect and honor me. You make space for and nurture my fullest expression even and especially when I'm at my worst. I am a better person for loving and being loved by you.

Girlfriends, thank you for easing my heart, bringing laughter to my life, and "making me" have fun. Thank you for sharing your tears, holding me tight, calling me on my crap, and putting up with my not so humble opinions, especially Stella who somehow managed to stick close through 287 months and counting. And Max, in spite of your penis, you're a tried a true girlfriend. And sweet Martha for knowing me the best.

I also want to thank those of you who shared your own births with me: Mom, Emma, Stella, and the incredible women of Northern Uganda* who welcomed me into your home and allowed me to serve you.

And to the midwives: no job demands so much, pays so little, and has been persecuted by so many. Still, you serve. Of course, I hold special love for those who supported me in labor: Laura, Laureen, Veege, Rhione, and Stella.

To those who work to protect the sanctity of birth, especially you who believed in and endorsed my work even before the agents and publisher did: Dr. Christiane Northrup, Dr. Marsden Wagner, and Hermine Hayes-Klein.

To my employees, past and present, you rock! Pangea would not be what it is without you. You do so much more than work hard and nourish thousands of people a year. You are the heart and soul of Pangea. Thank you.

To those who have helped me face fear and work for my heart's desire, especially Julie Goodnight, Rachel Zaslow, Olivia Kimball, T. Harv, Greg and Kourosh; and Steve Harrison, Geoffrey Berwind, and the rest of the team at Bradley Communications.

And to those who helped heal me: Elizabeth Robinson, Dianne O., Karen H., Lee S., David M., and YMG.

---

* To learn more about Roanna's time volunteering in Uganda, visit www.cut-stapledandmended.com/bonus.

To those who helped grow this book: Mom, Eliza Greenwood, Stella Lynn, Laura Roe, and William Kowalski all read and re-read drafts, challenged me to improve upon it, to go deeper and say more. You were relentless. That's a compliment. And to Carolyn Bond who, in addition to the above, ruthlessly chopped away the bits that I thought I loved most. That's a compliment also.

To Christy Collins for, in spite of my attempts to help, creating the most beautiful cover ever for me. And to Steven Scholl and Stephen Sendar who were willing to compromise and meet me in the middle of a most unusual publishing contract, thereby allowing me to birth *Cut, Stapled and Mended* on my own terms.

But most of all, I want to thank **you**, the reader, for bearing witness.

Readers' Discussion Guide

Chapter 1: She Visits

1. Roanna claims to reject her parent's New Age and food ideologies. Do you see any contradiction between her claim and her actions?

2. Are there beliefs or practices from your own childhood that you tried to dismiss but, in retrospect, continue to intertwine throughout your life?

Chapter 2: Baby Dreams

1. How was Roanna's desire to have a baby as a "responsible adult" different than her desire to do so as a "rebellious teen"?

2. What does Ben and Roanna's choice to leave South Florida, in spite of family resistance and their opening their own cafe in spite of their lack of experience founding or managing businesses, say about them? How might this foreshadow their birth experiences?

Chapter 3: Herstory

1. How does Laureen's midwifery care compare to what you have experienced, or what you expect, maternity care to be?

2. Roanna correlates her decision to go live in her father's home to the way she herself was born. Thinking about the circumstances surrounding your own birth, are there decisions or ways of being that might reflect your own entry into the world?

Chapter 4: Blessing Way

1. How far back can you name your maternal lineage? What do you know about these women?

2. Do you think Roanna is seeking or resisting the feminine?

Chapter 5: My Sun

1. How does Roanna's cesarean compare to the often-repeated idea that cesareans deliveries are easier than vaginal deliveries? Though she doesn't describe the surgery as painful, are the other things she reveals worth the absence of pain?

2. Roanna does not question her treatment, unnecessary ultrasound, the cesarean, or her separation from her baby. Instead she orders a dessert tray to thank the staff for "doing all of the things mothers should be able to do but I cannot." Do you feel the staff was worthy of this gift?

Chapter 6: Nummie Woman

1. Roanna is haunted by the memory of "failing" her son. Since he won't remember his birth, does this really matter?

2. Contrary to the FDA and the drug-makers warnings, Cytotec continues to be used to induce labor. What does this say about our birth system?

Chapter 7: Snake Oil

1. Roanna says "It would be so much easier if I could stop thinking and questioning, if I could simply accept and believe, if I could learn to 'baaaa.'" Is there anything in your own life you feel this way about?

2. Does the replacement of the word "contractions" with "surges" and "pain" with "pressure" change the way you think of these experiences? Can you think of other common words or expressions that might be served to change?

Chapter 8: The Window

1. How does Dr. Vikson's manner of care influence Roanna's experience of her second cesarean?

2. This time, Roanna "chooses numbness." Why didn't she do so after the first cesarean? Is numbness a healthier response than her response to the first cesarean?

Chapter 9: The Lie

1. Roanna is very relieved that "in spite of the events surrounding Jonah's birth, she [Dr. Vikson] doesn't dislike me." Why does Roanna feel the need to please Dr. Vikson? Under what other circumstances does the drive to please someone who we hire, instead of expecting that they please us, occur?

2. Were the hospital rules about VBAC reasonable? Under what circumstances is it acceptable to force a woman to receive unwanted surgery?

Chapter 10: Eve's Truth

1. What was the first story or explanation you heard about birth? Has this story influenced your subsequent choices, experiences, or beliefs surrounding childbirth?

2. Do you know the story of your own birth? Do you believe your birth was an isolated experience or has it continued to unwind throughout your life?

Chapter 11: She Returns

1. What's on your "someday list" and what truly stops you from doing it?

2. Roanna partially blames her "prickly and defensive" behavior on other's expectations that she behave this way. Do other's expectations set you up for certain behaviors?

Chapter 12: Ring of Fire

1. Roanna has a strong desire to not disappoint her doctor. Is this based on respect for her, discomfort at possibly being found out, fear of retribution or . . . .?

2. For the first time, Roanna talks not about avoiding a cesarean but about craving to experience birth. What is the significance of this?

Chapter 13: Merbaby

1. Roanna refers to god as feminine. How does it sit with you?

2. Roanna is far from brave in this chapter, even admitting that if a stranger walked in and offered her a cesarean, she would accept it. Because she was at home, this wasn't an option for her. But in a hospital, it might be. How should providers balance a woman's pre-labor birth plans with their wishes during labor?

Chapter 14: Amaryllis and Dalia

1. Placenta Soup: Could you? Would you? Why is food from one's own body largely viewed with such resistance?

2. Though clearly traumatized by birth, Roanna also doesn't want to let it go, describing the recovery as "I am, once again, mortal." How can both be true? Does Roanna's telling make natural childbirth a more or less desirable experience?

Chapter 15: Bunk Beds

1. Roanna claims that all she wanted to do was give birth but instead found herself transformed. Do you think this was the result of giving birth? Or was giving birth naturally the result of her transformation?

2. On the cover of *Cut, Stapled, & Mended*, Dr. Marsden Wagner, former director of Women's and Children's Health at the World Health Organization says that this book needs to be read, not just by pregnant and to-be pregnant women, but also by to-be fathers, midwives, nurses, hospital administrators and, most especially, by doctors. But this book offers little information about techniques, tools, or education for birth attendants. Do you think it's important for birth attendants to expose themselves to stories like this or is it better for them to keep an emotional distance?

About the Author

Roanna Rosewood is an international award-winning speaker, successful restaurateur, accomplished real estate investor, co-founder of BirthPlan Radio, and most importantly, a mother. In her not-so-humble opinion, the latter makes her a true birth expert. "It's time to put women's needs, feelings, and intuition back in the center of the birth process. Women are the rock-stars of birth; professionals are the backup singers."
Roanna attributes her ability to give birth naturally in spite of two previous cesareans and the "fact" that her pelvis was "too small," to taking back her rightful place in birth. Helping others regain theirs is her passion in life.

More information on Roanna and her work can be found at the following website: www.RoannaRosewood.com